Euthanasia

OPPOSING VIEWPOINTS®

OTHER BOOKS OF RELATED INTEREST

OPPOSING VIEWPOINTS SERIES

Abortion
Death and Dying
The Death Penalty
Opposing Viewpoints in Social Issues
Suicide

CURRENT CONTROVERSIES SERIES

The Abortion Controversy
Assisted Suicide
Capital Punishment
Medical Ethics

AT ISSUE SERIES

Does Capital Punishment Deter Crime?
The Ethics of Euthanasia
Physician-Assisted Suicide

Euthanasia

OPPOSING VIEWPOINTS ®

James D. Torr, Book Editor

David L. Bender, Publisher
Bruno Leone, Executive Editor
Bonnie Szumski, Editorial Director
David M. Haugen, Managing Editor

OPPOSING
VIEWPOINTS ®
SERIES

Greenhaven Press, Inc., San Diego, California

Cover photo: Corbis Images

Library of Congress Cataloging-in-Publication Data

Euthanasia : opposing viewpoints / James D. Torr, editor.
    p.   cm.
   Includes bibliographical references and index.
   ISBN 0-7377-0126-9 (pbk. : alk. paper). —
ISBN 0-7377-0127-7 (lib. : alk. paper)
   1. Euthanasia. 2. Assisted suicide. 3. Medical ethics. I. Torr, James,
1974–   .
R726.E7924 2000
179.7—dc21   99-16488
                                                                              CIP

Greenhaven Press, Inc., P.O. Box 289009
San Diego, CA 92198-9009

"CONGRESS SHALL MAKE NO LAW...ABRIDGING THE FREEDOM OF SPEECH, OR OF THE PRESS."

First Amendment to the U.S. Constitution

The basic foundation of our democracy is the First Amendment guarantee of freedom of expression. The Opposing Viewpoints Series is dedicated to the concept of this basic freedom and the idea that it is more important to practice it than to enshrine it.

CONTENTS

WHY CONSIDER OPPOSING VIEWPOINTS?

"The only way in which a human being can make some approach to knowing the whole of a subject is by hearing what can be said about it by persons of every variety of opinion and studying all modes in which it can be looked at by every character of mind. No wise man ever acquired his wisdom in any mode but this."

John Stuart Mill

In our media-intensive culture it is not difficult to find differing opinions. Thousands of newspapers and magazines and dozens of radio and television talk shows resound with differing points of view. The difficulty lies in deciding which opinion to agree with and which "experts" seem the most credible. The more inundated we become with differing opinions and claims, the more essential it is to hone critical reading and thinking skills to evaluate these ideas. Opposing Viewpoints books address this problem directly by presenting stimulating debates that can be used to enhance and teach these skills. The varied opinions contained in each book examine many different aspects of a single issue. While examining these conveniently edited opposing views, readers can develop critical thinking skills such as the ability to compare and contrast authors' credibility, facts, argumentation styles, use of persuasive techniques, and other stylistic tools. In short, the Opposing Viewpoints Series is an ideal way to attain the higher-level thinking and reading skills so essential in a culture of diverse and contradictory opinions.

In addition to providing a tool for critical thinking, Opposing Viewpoints books challenge readers to question their own strongly held opinions and assumptions. Most people form their opinions on the basis of upbringing, peer pressure, and personal, cultural, or professional bias. By reading carefully balanced opposing views, readers must directly confront new ideas as well as the opinions of those with whom they disagree. This is not to simplistically argue that everyone who reads opposing views will—or should—change his or her opinion. Instead, the series enhances readers' understanding of their own views by encouraging confrontation with opposing ideas. Careful examination of others' views can lead to the readers' understanding of the logical inconsistencies in their own opinions, perspective on why they hold an opinion, and the consideration of the possibility that their opinion requires further evaluation.

Evaluating Other Opinions

To ensure that this type of examination occurs, Opposing Viewpoints books present all types of opinions. Prominent spokespeople on different sides of each issue as well as well-known professionals from many disciplines challenge the reader. An additional goal of the series is to provide a forum for other, less known, or even unpopular viewpoints. The opinion of an ordinary person who has had to make the decision to cut off life support from a terminally ill relative, for example, may be just as valuable and provide just as much insight as a medical ethicist's professional opinion. The editors have two additional purposes in including these less known views. One, the editors encourage readers to respect others' opinions—even when not enhanced by professional credibility. It is only by reading or listening to and objectively evaluating others' ideas that one can determine whether they are worthy of consideration. Two, the inclusion of such viewpoints encourages the important critical thinking skill of objectively evaluating an author's credentials and bias. This evaluation will illuminate an author's reasons for taking a particular stance on an issue and will aid in readers' evaluation of the author's ideas.

As series editors of the Opposing Viewpoints Series, it is our hope that these books will give readers a deeper understanding of the issues debated and an appreciation of the complexity of even seemingly simple issues when good and honest people disagree. This awareness is particularly important in a democratic society such as ours in which people enter into public debate to determine the common good. Those with whom one disagrees should not be regarded as enemies but rather as people whose views deserve careful examination and may shed light on one's own.

Thomas Jefferson once said that "difference of opinion leads to inquiry, and inquiry to truth." Jefferson, a broadly educated man, argued that "if a nation expects to be ignorant and free . . . it expects what never was and never will be." As individuals and as a nation, it is imperative that we consider the opinions of others and examine them with skill and discernment. The Opposing Viewpoints Series is intended to help readers achieve this goal.

David L. Bender & Bruno Leone,
Series Editors

Greenhaven Press anthologies primarily consist of previously published material taken from a variety of sources, including periodicals, books, scholarly journals, newspapers, government documents, and position papers from private and public organizations. These original sources are often edited for length and to ensure their accessibility for a young adult audience. The anthology editors also change the original titles of these works in order to clearly present the main thesis of each viewpoint and to explicitly indicate the opinion presented in the viewpoint. These alterations are made in consideration of both the reading and comprehension levels of a young adult audience. Every effort is made to ensure that Greenhaven Press accurately reflects the original intent of the authors included in this anthology.

INTRODUCTION

"Death is not the worst evil, but rather when we wish to die and cannot."

Sophocles (496–406 B.C.)

"Euthanasia" is a broad term for mercy killing—taking the life of a hopelessly ill or injured individual in order to end his or her suffering. Mercy killing represents a serious ethical dilemma. People do not always die well. Some afflictions cause people to suffer through extreme physical pain in their last days, and euthanasia may seem like a compassionate way of ending this pain. Other patients may request euthanasia to avoid the weakness and loss of mental faculties that some diseases cause, and many feel these wishes should be respected.

But euthanasia also seems to contradict one of the most basic principles of morality, which is that killing is wrong. Viewed from a traditional Judeo-Christian point of view, euthanasia is murder and a blatant violation of the biblical commandment "Thou shalt not kill." From a secular perspective, one of the principal purposes of law is to uphold the sanctity of human life. Euthanasia is so controversial because it pits the plight of suffering, dying individuals against religious beliefs, legal tradition, and, in the case of physician-assisted death, medical ethics.

This moral dilemma is not new. The term "euthanasia" is derived from ancient Greek, and means "good death." But while the debate over mercy killing has ancient origins, many observers believe that it is harder today to achieve a good death than ever before. Advances in medicine have increased people's health and life span, but they have also greatly affected the dying process. For example, in the early twentieth century the majority of Americans died at home, usually victims of pneumonia or influenza. Today most people die in the hospital, often from degenerative diseases like cancer that may cause a painful, lingering death.

Most observers trace the modern euthanasia debate back to the court case of Karen Ann Quinlan, and her story is a poignant example of medical technology's ability to prolong life. In 1975, after consuming alcohol and tranquilizers at a party, Quinlan collapsed into an irreversible coma that left her unable to breathe without a respirator or eat without a feeding tube. Her parents asked that she be removed from the respirator, but her doctors objected. The New Jersey Supreme Court case that followed was the first to bring the issue of euthanasia into the public eye. In 1976 the court allowed Quinlan's parents to have the respirator removed. Although Quinlan lived for another nine years (her parents did not want her feeding tube removed), the case set a precedent for a patient's right to refuse unwanted medical treatment.

In 1990, this right was further expanded in the case of Nancy Cruzan. Cruzan had gone into an irreversible coma in 1983 after a severe car crash, and her parents wanted the machine that was keeping her alive removed. However, in this case the machine consisted of intravenous feeding tubes that provided Cruzan with hydration and nutrition. Her parents viewed the removal of the machine as the termination of unwanted treatment. However, the state of Missouri argued that to remove the feeding tubes would be to intentionally kill Cruzan through starvation. In a controversial vote, the U.S. Supreme Court ruled that the provision of artificially delivered food and water is a treatment which patients may legally refuse, even if doing so will result in death.

The cases of Quinlan and Cruzan helped develop a social policy that recognizes that some lifesaving treatments are not always appropriate, and permits the removal of these treatments as a form of "passive" euthanasia. But shortly after the Cruzan case more active forms of euthanasia became the focus of public attention. One of the persons most responsible for this is Timothy E. Quill, a physician who in 1991 described in the *New England Journal of Medicine* the case of "Diane," a longtime patient of his who was suffering from acute leukemia. She asked Quill for the means to end her life should she find it intolerable, and, unable to dissuade her, he prescribed sleeping pills, telling her how many were necessary to cure insomnia and how many were necessary to commit suicide. Four months later Diane killed herself.

Quill's article provoked immediate and heated discussion over the legality of physicians' assisting in suicide. Quill's self-proclaimed goal is to improve the care dying people receive rather than to legalize any form of euthanasia. Nevertheless, he became a central figure in a court case that challenged the constitutionality of state bans on assisted suicide—Quill and other right-to-die advocates essentially argued that terminally ill patients have a constitutional right to assisted suicide. In 1997, however, the Supreme Court disagreed, ruling that states may legislate for or against physician-assisted suicide as they see fit. (Currently, over 35 states have laws against assisted suicide; only Oregon has legalized the practice.)

Ironically, however, the person most responsible for bringing euthanasia into the public eye is one from whom most right-to-die activists have tried to distance themselves: former pathologist Jack Kevorkian, who has admitted helping over 130 people die since 1990. Whereas Quill is regarded as a reasoned, thoughtful spokesman for the terminally ill, Kevorkian is seen as a renegade. Many of the people he has helped to die were not terminally ill, and he did not know them before they requested his assistance in suicide. He holds some bizarre opinions: In his book *Prescription: Medicide*, Kevorkian advocates experimentation on patients before they die and nonvoluntary euthanasia for anyone whom physicians deem to have an extremely low quality of life. Many of his views and methods have been condemned by right-to-die leaders, yet Kevorkian is the name people most associate with euthanasia.

Prior to 1998, Kevorkian only assisted in suicides. He rigged so-called suicide machines that allowed patients to self-administer a lethal dose of drugs. However, on November 23, 1998, *60 Minutes* aired a videotape of Kevorkian participating in a more active form of euthanasia. For the first time, he administered the fatal injection himself, ending the life of Thomas Youk, a fifty-two-year-old who suffered from Lou Gehrig's disease. On March 26, 1999, a Michigan jury, faced with this videotape evidence, found Kevorkian guilty of murder. The judge in the case did not allow the defense to present testimony about Youk's pain and suffering, and emphasized that whether the victim consents is legally irrelevant in murder cases. Kevorkian plans to appeal the verdict.

Kevorkian's is the latest in a series of contentious euthanasia cases that have challenged and, in some cases, changed Americans' beliefs about death, mercy, and killing. Less than three decades ago, many people considered the removal of a comatose patient's respirator a shocking act of passive euthanasia. Today, the most divisive euthanasia cases concern physician-assisted suicide and Kevorkian's direct mercy killing. The authors in *Euthanasia: Opposing Viewpoints* debate these increasingly complex topics in the following chapters: Is Euthanasia Ethical? Should Voluntary Euthanasia Be Legalized? Would Legalizing Euthanasia Lead to Involuntary Killing? Should Physicians Assist in Suicide? The viewpoints in this book help shed light on the legal and ethical problems that Americans continue to face in their quest for a "good death."

CHAPTER 1

IS EUTHANASIA ETHICAL?

CHAPTER PREFACE

"Euthanasia" is a blanket term that can encompass a variety of situations, and many authors use the term to mean different things. For example, some view physician-assisted suicide as a form of voluntary euthanasia, while others treat it as a separate issue. Others may distinguish between "active" euthanasia, or killing, and "passive" euthanasia, or allowing to die. Because of these different connotations, it is important to be aware of how the term is being used in a given context. Andrew Solomon, writing in the May 22, 1995, *New Yorker*, sums up the several distinctions that experts make when discussing euthanasia, listing them in order of least to most controversial:

> There are essentially six degrees of euthanasia under discussion in the United States. The most basic is discontinuing artificial life-support systems (ventilators, shunts, etc.) for a patient in an irreversible coma who cannot live without such intervention. The second is discontinuing feeding or hydration for a comatose patient who does not require any other artificial support. The third is withholding (at the patient's request) treatment that can extend the life of but not cure a severely or terminally ill patient. The fourth is providing pain relief to someone in great pain knowing that the pain medication may hasten that patient's death (the double effect). The fifth is giving a patient access to means that the patient may use to kill himself in order to escape from severe or terminal illness. The sixth is administering a lethal injection (at the patient's request) to a patient who is severely or terminally ill. Involuntary euthanasia, which occurs when someone takes it upon himself to "put out of his pain" a patient without that patient's explicit knowledge or consent, is outside the dominant American dialogue.

Many people believe that some of these forms of euthanasia are permissible in certain circumstances, but that others are always immoral. Thus, few advocates on either side of the issue contend that it is absolutely wrong or right. Instead, the authors in the following chapter debate where the moral line should be drawn among Solomon's six degrees of euthanasia.

"Not everyone wants a lingering death."

VOLUNTARY EUTHANASIA IS ETHICAL

Derek Humphry

In the following viewpoint, Derek Humphry argues that euthanasia is ethically justified as a means of relieving unbearable suffering, as long as it is limited to fully informed adults who specifically request it. Humphry maintains that decisions about dying are highly personal and that euthanasia should not be denied to those who choose it. Humphry, the founder of the Hemlock Society and subsequently the Euthanasia Research and Guidance Organization, has written several books on euthanasia, including Final Exit: The Practicalities of Self-Deliverance and Assisted Suicide and Dying with Dignity: Understanding Euthanasia.

As you read, consider the following questions:

1. What term does Humphry prefer for what he deems "justifiable suicide"?
2. In the author's view, what are the two situations in which euthanasia can be ethical?
3. What point do hospice leaders miss, in Humphry's opinion?

Reprinted from Derek Humphry, "Why I Believe in Voluntary Euthanasia," 1995 Euthanasia Research & Guidance Organization, (ERGO!) website article at www.finalexit.org, by permission of author.

The Euthanasia Research & Guidance Organization (ERGO!) is dedicated to the view that there are at least two forms of suicide. One is 'emotional suicide,' or irrational self-murder in all of it complexities and sadness. Let me emphasize at once that ERGO's view of this tragic form of self-destruction is the same as that of the suicide intervention movement and the rest of society, which is to prevent it wherever possible. We do not support any form of suicide for mental health or emotional reasons.

JUSTIFIABLE SUICIDE

But we do say that there is a second form of suicide—justifiable suicide, that is, rational and planned self-deliverance from a painful and hopeless disease which will shortly end in death. I don't think the word 'suicide' sits well in this context but we are stuck with it. I have struggled for twenty years to popularize the term 'self-deliverance' but it is an uphill battle because the news media is in love with the words 'assisted suicide.' Also, we have to face the fact that the law calls all forms of self-destruction 'suicide.'

Let me point out here for those who might not know it that suicide is no longer a crime anywhere in the English-speaking world. (It used to be, and was punishable by giving all the dead person's money and goods to the government.) Attempted suicide is no longer a crime, although under health laws a person can in most states be forcibly placed in a psychiatric hospital for three days for evaluation.

But giving assistance in suicide remains a crime, except in the Netherlands in recent times under certain conditions, and it has never been a crime in Switzerland, Germany, Norway and Uruguay. The rest of the world punishes assistance in suicide for both the mentally ill and the terminally ill, although the American state of Oregon recently (Nov. 1994) passed by ballot Measure 16, a limited physician-assisted suicide law.

Even if a hopelessly ill person is requesting assistance in dying for the most compassionate reasons, and the helper is acting from the most noble of motives, it remains a crime in the Anglo-American world. Punishments range from fines to fourteen years in prison. It is this catch-all prohibition which ERGO! and other right-to-die groups wish to change. In a caring society, under the rule of law, we claim that there must be exceptions.

ACHIEVING A GOOD DEATH

The word 'euthanasia' comes from the Greek—eu, "good," and thanatos, "death." Literally, "good death." But the word 'euthanasia' has acquired a more complex meaning in modern times. It is generally taken nowadays to mean doing something about achieving a good death.

Suicide, self-deliverance, auto-euthanasia, aid-in-dying, assisted suicide—call it what you like—can be justified by the average supporter of the so-called 'right to die' movement for the following reasons:

1. Advanced terminal illness that is causing unbearable suffering to the individual. This is the most common reason to seek an early end.

2. Grave physical handicap which is so restricting that the individual cannot, even after due consideration, counseling and re-training, tolerate such a limited existence. This is a fairly rare reason for suicide—most impaired people cope remarkably well with their affliction—but there are some who would, at a certain point, rather die.

ETHICAL PARAMETERS

What are the ethical parameters for euthanasia?

1. The person is a mature adult. This is essential. The exact age will depend on the individual but the person should not be a minor, who comes under quite different laws.

2. The person has clearly made a considered decision. An individual has the ability nowadays to indicate this with a "Living Will" (which applies only to disconnection of life supports) and can also, in today's more open and tolerant climate about such actions, freely discuss the option of euthanasia with health professionals, family, lawyers, etc.

3. The euthanasia has not been carried out at the first knowledge of a life-threatening illness, and reasonable medical help has been sought to cure or at least slow down the terminal disease. We do not believe in giving up life the minute a person is informed that he or she has a terminal illness. (This is a common misconception spread by our critics.) Life is precious, you only pass this way once, and is worth a fight. It is when the fight is clearly hopeless and the agony, physical and mental, is unbearable that a final exit is an option.

4. The treating physician has been informed, asked to be involved, and his or her response been taken into account. What the physician's response will be depends on the circumstances, of course, but we advise people that as rational suicide is not a crime, there is nothing a doctor can do about it. But it is best to inform the doctor and hear his or her response. For example, the patient might be mistaken—perhaps the diagnosis has been misheard or misunderstood. It used to be that patients raising

this subject were met with a discreet silence, or meaningless remarks, but in today's more accepting climate most physicians will discuss potential end of life actions.

5. The person has made a Will disposing of his or her worldly effects and money. This shows evidence of a tidy mind, an orderly life, and forethought—all something which is paramount to an acceptance of rational suicide.

6. The person has made plans to exit that do not involve others in criminal liability or leave them with guilt feelings. As I have mentioned earlier, assistance in suicide is a crime in most places, although the laws are gradually changing, and very few cases ever came before the courts. But care must still be taken and discretion is the watchword.

7. The person leaves a note saying exactly why he or she is taking their life. This statement in writing obviates the chance of subsequent misunderstandings or blame. It also demonstrates that the departing person is taking full responsibility for the action.

NOT ALWAYS NOTICED

A great many cases of self-deliverance or assisted suicide, using drugs and/or a plastic bag, go undetected by doctors, especially now that autopsies are the exception rather than the rule (only 10 percent, and only when there is a mystery about the cause of death). Also, if a doctor asked for a death certificate knows that the patient was in advanced terminal illness then he is not going to be too concerned about the precise cause of death. It hardly matters.

I find that police, paramedics and coroners put a very low priority of investigation of suicide when evidence comes before them that the person was dying anyway, and there is a note from the deceased. Detectives and coroners' officers will walk away from the scene once they are satisfied that the person who committed suicide was terminally ill.

But, having considered the logic in favor of auto-euthanasia, the person should also contemplate the arguments against it.

QUALITY OF LIFE CONSIDERATIONS

First, should the person go instead into a hospice program and receive not only first-class pain management but comfort care and personal attention? Put bluntly, hospices make the best of a bad job, and they do so with great skill and love. The right-to-die movement supports their work. But not everyone wants a lingering death, not everyone wants that form of care. Today many terminally ill people take the marvellous benefits of home hospice programs and still accelerate the end when suffering becomes too much.

A few hospice leaders claim that their care is so perfect that there is absolutely no need for anyone to consider euthanasia. While I have no wish to criticize them, they are wrong to claim perfection. Most, but not all, terminal pain can today be controlled with the sophisticated use of drugs, but the point these leaders miss is that *personal quality of life* is vital to some people. If one's body has been so destroyed by disease that it is not worth living, that is an intensely individual decision which should not be thwarted. In some cases of the final days in hospice care, when the pain is very serious, the patient is drugged into unconsciousness. If that way is acceptable to the patient, fine. But some people do not wish their final hours to be in that fashion.

There should be no conflict between hospice and euthanasia—both are valid options in a caring society. Both are appropriate to different people with differing values.

RELIGIOUS OBJECTIONS TO EUTHANASIA

The other consideration is theological: does suffering ennoble? Is suffering, and relating to Jesus Christ's suffering on the cross, a part of preparation for meeting God? Are you merely a steward of your life, which is a gift from God, which only He may take away? My response is this: if your answers to these questions are yes, then you should not be involved in any form of euthanasia.

But remember that there are millions of atheists and agnostics, as well as people of varieties of religions, degrees of spiritual beliefs, and they all have rights, too. Many Christians who believe in euthanasia justify it by reasoning that the God whom they worship is loving and tolerant, and would not wish to see them in agony. They do not see their God as being so vengeful as refusing them the Kingdom of Heaven if they accelerated the end of their life to avoid prolonged, unbearable suffering.

Another consideration must be that, by checking out before the Grim Reaper calls, is one is depriving oneself of a valuable period of good life? Is that last period of love and companionship with family and friends worth hanging on for? The argument that this is so is heavily used by our critics.

But in my twenty years in this movement, and being aware of many hundreds of self-deliverances, I can attest that even the most determined supporters of euthanasia hang on until the last minute—sometimes too long, and lose control. They, too, gather with their families and friends to say goodbyes. There are important reunions and often farewell parties.

Euthanasia supporters enjoy life and love living, and their respect for the sanctity of life is as strong as anybody's. Yet they are willing, if their dying is distressing to them, to forgo a few weeks or a few days at the very end and leave under their own control.

KNOWLEDGE IS COMFORT

What many people do not realize is that, for many people, just knowing how to kill themselves is in itself of great comfort. It gives them the assurance to fight harder and therefore often extends lives just a bit longer. Many people have remarked to me that my book, Final Exit, is "the best insurance policy I've ever taken out." Once such people know how to make a certain and dignified self-deliverance, they will often renegotiate the timing of their death.

Recently a man in his 90s called up and told me his health was so bad he was ready to terminate his life. I advised him to read Final Exit, which he did and he called me back. He had managed to get hold of lethal drugs from a friendly doctor and so everything was in position.

"So what are you going to do now?" I asked him.

"Oh, I'm not ready to go yet," he replied. "I've got the means, so I can hold on a bit longer."

Now that he had the knowledge and the drugs, with control and choice in his grasp, he had negotiated new terms with himself concerning his fate. Surely, for those who want it this way, this is commendable and is in fact an extension rather than a curtailment of life. What is needed now are careful laws permitting physician-assisted suicide—voluntary on everybody's part. The new Oregon Death with Dignity Act is a beginning.

"All killing of patients is morally wrong, while allowing some patients to die is not."

VOLUNTARY EUTHANASIA IS UNETHICAL

Daniel P. Sulmasy

In the following viewpoint, Daniel P. Sulmasy, a Franciscan monk and professor of medicine at the Center for Clinical Bioethics at Georgetown University in Washington, D.C., argues that euthanasia is wrong because it is the act of killing another person. The author does not believe that dying patients must be kept alive at all costs; on the contrary, Sulmasy contends that it is sometimes ethical to stop a dying person's treatment and allow him or her to die. However, in the author's opinion, killing is always wrong because all human life has intrinsic value.

As you read, consider the following questions:

1. What does the Hippocratic Oath, as quoted by the author, say about patients who are "overmastered with disease"?
2. What, according to Sulmasy, is the key to understanding whether a given act of allowing to die is wrong?
3. In Sulmasy's opinion, what effect does the loss of freedom and control have on the value of a person's life?

Reprinted from Daniel P. Sulmasy, "Death with Dignity: A Franciscan Doctor's Perspective," St. Anthony Messenger, January 1996, by permission of author.

We live in a curious world. The most famous physician on the planet is now Dr. Jack Kevorkian, who makes a living helping people commit suicide. Efforts are afoot in several states to allow doctors legally to help kill their patients. In November of 1994, for example, with little fanfare, the voters of Oregon passed the world's first law to make it legal for doctors to help patients commit suicide. The law . . . requires doctors who participate to prescribe a "safe lethal dose." Questions about how a dose could be both safe and lethal at the same time seem to escape the authors of the bill. The world, as Alice in Wonderland once said, gets curiouser and curiouser.

Many people have become confused by this curious debate about physician-assisted suicide and euthanasia. Some have been led to believe (falsely) that they and their loved ones will be forced to make a cruel choice at the end of life: either languish for months on a torturous ventilator or swallow a few dozen pills and end it all. But this view is wrong—dead wrong. My aim in this article is to help explain the morality of allowing patients to die—a middle course between purposeless treatment on the one hand and euthanasia or suicide on the other.

Since most deaths in America are now preceded by a decision to withhold or withdraw some form of treatment, you probably have had personal experience here. My own grandfather died while I was an intern, just out of medical school. I helped my mother come to the decision not to put him on a ventilator and not to attempt cardiopulmonary resuscitation when his heart stopped. These decisions were hard ones, but they seemed morally correct, and were perfectly permissible under Church teaching. Yet it would not have seemed morally correct to have given my grandfather an injection of a rapidly acting poison. We let Poppy die, but we didn't kill him. What explains the moral difference between these two actions?

THE HIPPOCRATIC OATH AND CATHOLIC TRADITION

History can help to illuminate our question, but only if the historical facts are accurately understood. Unfortunately, many people (including many doctors) are confused about what ancient doctors like Hippocrates had to say about killing and allowing to die. The Hippocratic Oath is the traditional standard of medicine.

First, it is important to realize that the Hippocratic Oath does not say that physicians must continue to treat patients and keep them alive no matter what. The oath says, "I will use treatment to help the sick according to my ability and judgment." This clearly does not mean keep treating until the treatment kills the patient.

Second, Hippocrates also says that physicians should "refuse to treat those who are overmastered by their disease, realizing that in such cases medicine is powerless."

Third, the Oath of Hippocrates expressly prohibits euthanasia and assisted suicide, saying "I will not give poison to anyone though asked to do so, nor will I suggest such a plan." So, it seems fair to say that Hippocrates at least implicitly accepted the idea of a distinction between killing and allowing to die.

From the earliest days, Christians considered suicide and euthanasia sinful. However, by the 16th century, long before there were ventilators or intensive-care units, Catholic theologians developed the distinction between *ordinary* and *extraordinary* means. They taught that Christians had a moral obligation to preserve their lives in the face of illness, but that they were not required to go to extraordinary lengths to do so.

If a 16th-century doctor said that moving to the mountains would be best for a patient's health, and moving to the mountains would require leaving family and friends and losing the immediate family's savings, the patient was under no obligation to do so. Therefore, by the time there *were* things like ventilators around, it was easy for Pope Pius XII to say in 1957 that such treatments might present the patient with an "extraordinary" burden, and it would therefore be morally permissible to forgo such treatment.

Thus the Church distinguished clearly between killing patients by suicide or euthanasia (which has never been permissible), and allowing them to die by withholding or withdrawing life-supporting treatments (which has been seen as permissible in the right circumstances).

KILLING VERSUS ALLOWING TO DIE

Philosophers have recently attacked this distinction between killing and allowing to die, arguing that it is unsound. Some of their arguments have helped to make matters clearer. Others have left the picture even more confused.

One might be tempted to say that the difference between killing and allowing to die lies in the fact that killing is always active while allowing to die is always passive. Yet most people would agree that disconnecting a dying patient from a ventilator—an *act*—is a classical case of allowing to die. One actively turns off a switch or actively *disconnects* a piece of tubing. So the difference between killing and allowing to die can't just be the

26

difference between active and passive.

Second, one might suggest that, in killing, *a person* causes the patient's death, but in allowing to die *nature* causes the death. But it is hard to say that the one who disconnects a life-support system is not in some sense causing death. If the patient needs a continuous infusion of a medicine to maintain blood pressure, and the doctor turns a stopcock, the medicine stops, the blood pressure drops, and the patient goes into shock and dies, can the doctor seriously claim to have played no causal role in the death?

Smith and Jones

Even if one could adequately describe the difference between killing and allowing to die, it is argued, the distinction wouldn't make a *moral* difference. Let me illustrate my point with two case studies from philosopher and euthanasia proponent James Rachels:

"Smith stands to gain a large inheritance if anything should happen to his six-year-old cousin. One evening while the child is taking his bath, Smith sneaks into the bathroom and drowns the child, and then arranges things to make it look like an accident. No one is the wiser, and Smith gets his inheritance.

"Jones also stands to gain if anything should happen to his six-year-old cousin. Like Smith, Jones sneaks in planning to drown the child in his bath. However, just as he enters the bathroom Jones sees the child slip, hit his head and fall face-down in the water. Jones is delighted; he stands by, ready to push the child's head back down under if necessary, but it is not necessary. With only a little thrashing about, the child drowns all by himself, 'accidentally,' as Jones watches and does nothing. No one is the wiser, and Jones gets his inheritance."

So, it seems as if Smith killed his cousin and Jones allowed his cousin to die. But, Rachels asks, does this make a moral difference? He would answer no.

Distinctions Are Critical

I want to argue that there is an important logical mistake in Rachels's question. He would be right (there would be no moral distinction) if you could agree that all acts of killing are morally wrong, and all acts of allowing to die are morally right. But that's not what either traditional medicine or Catholic teaching holds. Catholic understanding makes distinctions among situations where death is imminent. Catholic understanding would say it like this: All acts of killing patients are morally wrong. Some acts of allowing them to die are also morally wrong, and some are not.

Once one understands the distinction between killing and allowing to die, the stories of Smith and Jones can be seen as illustrations of the distinction, not as a refutation. All acts of killing are morally wrong, and so Smith is clearly wrong. Some acts of allowing to die are morally wrong, and some are not. Jones's story just falls into the category of acts of allowing to die that are morally wrong. That's plain to see.

Here is how I would phrase the distinction between killing and allowing to die: *Killing is an act in which someone performs an action that gives the victim a new fatal disease with the intention of thereby causing the patient's death. Allowing to die is an act in which someone either performs an action to remove a treatment for a pre-existing fatal disease or refrains from action that would treat a pre-existing fatal disease.*

If I kill a patient by a lethal injection, I act and create a new and fatal disease that the patient didn't have before. If I do so intending that the patient should die as a result, that is always wrong. If I allow that same person to die (whether by removing ventilator treatment for a fatal disease called respiratory failure, or by refraining from starting ventilator treatment), this is sometimes wrong and sometimes right. Each instance requires careful consideration.

INTENTION IS THE KEY

What, then, explains the wrongness that all acts of killing patients have in common with the wrong acts of allowing to die? The answer is one word: intention. Anyone who kills a patient intends that the patient should die by way of that action. This is what makes killing wrong. If one allows a patient to die with the specific intention that the patient should die by way of that action (the patient might have lived otherwise), this is also wrong. This allowing to die is not to be confused with allowing a natural death, as we will see below.

In killing (or in physician-assisted suicide), the doctor intends the death of the patient. Just as Smith acts wrongly by drowning his cousin, so does the physician who gives a lethal injection. Nonetheless, some acts of allowing to die are also morally wrong—those in which the doctor's intention is the death of the patient.

So, for example, because Jones intends that his cousin should die in order for him to collect the inheritance, Jones is morally in the wrong. In the same way, if a doctor disconnects the ventilator from a patient with the explicit intention that the patient should die so that he and the patient's wife can run off together with the insurance money, that physician has also acted wrongly.

On the other hand, if the doctor disconnects the ventilator intending simply that the patient should not be on the ventilator (perhaps because it is useless in preventing inevitable death), that physician has *not* acted wrongly. This is *good* allowing to die. It is perfectly morally permissible.

KNOWING INTENTIONS

Intention plays a key role here, as it does in much of morality. But intentions, of course, are hard to know. Sometimes one does not even understand one's own intentions. And it is precisely because intentions are so difficult to know that the distinction between killing and allowing to die is so important.

Killing is usually easy to recognize. Injecting poison into a patient's veins is a pretty straightforward act. It would be hard to argue that one's intentions did not include the death of the patient if one were to inject a poison. The burden of proof is overwhelmingly on a killer to explain how it was a mistake (or the killer was deceived or drugged) so that the action would not really be intentional. It is therefore very useful to be able to distinguish acts of killing from acts of allowing to die: We know that killing, in the case of physicians treating patients, is always wrong.

This is not the case with allowing to die. If I unplug a ventilator, how does anyone know what my intentions were? It might even be hard for me to know. Nonetheless, one can apply a simple (if imperfect) check on one's intentions. One can ask, how would one feel if the patient were not to die after one's action? Would one feel that one had failed to accomplish what one had set out to do? Or would one be open to the possibility that the patient might survive? If one's honest answer is that one would not feel frustrated, but would be open to the possibility that the patient might survive, then the patient's death was probably not one's intention.

Consider the paradigm case of allowing to die: turning off the ventilator for Karen Ann Quinlan. As is well known, Ms. Quinlan did not die when her family finally won the court's approval and turned off the ventilator, even though her death was expected. But no one then tried to strangle her. Their intention was simply that Karen's death not be prevented by a ventilator. As it turned out, the ventilator was not preventing her death. She lived on for several years.

INTENTION ISN'T DESIRE

It is particularly important not to confuse desire with intention. Many who object to moral arguments based upon intentions have mistaken *intention* for *desire*. To show why intending something is not the same as desiring it, consider some examples. I can, for instance, intend to do what I do not desire (for example, going to see my patients when I am tired and would rather not). I can also desire to do what I do not intend (I may desire to eat a high-cholesterol diet but never form an intention to act that way lest my patients think me a hypocrite). Desiring something is not the same as intending to make it happen.

Reprinted by permission of Chuck Asay and Creators Syndicate.

Nor should one feel guilty about wanting loved ones to pass away quickly when they are close to death and suffering. I, for one, have certainly desired that some of my patients would die quickly after I have withdrawn life support. In many cases I have hoped for their quick death; even prayed that God would take them. But this does not mean that I *intended* their death. Yes, I desired their hasty death, but the taking of the life was God's.

Medicine has traditionally prohibited the intentional death of patients. But medicine does not want patients to be prisoners of technology. The traditional morality that has permitted withholding and withdrawing "extraordinary" care *presupposes* this distinction between killing and allowing to die. Patients should not suffer needlessly. If the treatment is of no benefit, or if the burdens of treatment are disproportionate to the expected benefits, one may withhold or withdraw that treatment. But the intention in doing so must simply be that the useless or burdensome treatment be withdrawn. What one cannot intend is that there should be no such human life.

WHY IS INTENDING DEATH WRONG?

Christians recognize life as a gift from God. Human life, taking God as its image and likeness, has a special worth or dignity. Believing that life has such dignity, one can never hold the destruction of that dignity as one's intention.

There was once a time when human life had intrinsic meaning; its value seemed intuitively obvious even to nonbelievers. Such a moral intuition can no longer be taken for granted.

One can argue that, without religion, human beings are inherently communal beings. The value of human life is held in trust by a web of relationships. One can therefore argue that suicide is a rejection of relationships—a violent severing of one's connections with one's fellow human beings.

Some might make the claim that life loses its value when freedom and control are gone. But every human life depends upon others, and that dependency does not diminish dignity. Some of the most important things about being human, like birth and mortality, are beyond human control. One cannot, by force of will, live a life free of all suffering.

One will never be able to choose one's biological parents, no matter how much success genetic engineering has. Further, human life does not appear to lose its value when freedom and control are taken away. One of my favorite portraits of dignity is a photo of the Rev. Dr. Martin Luther King, Jr., in an Alabama prison cell. Acts of injustice deny but cannot eradicate the intrinsic value of human life.

Of course, human meaning and value are not infinite. On a cosmic scale, human life seems small, frail and fallible. One need only believe that each human life has a high intrinsic value, and that this dignity is the same for everyone. The value of human life cannot be said to admit of degrees. To say so is to say that some people's lives are more valuable than others'. If all human lives have intrinsic meaning and value, then to intend someone's death is to deny that the dying person's life has such value. But humans are finite; death is a part of life. Since that person's value is not infinite, one can sometimes let go of that life by allowing to die. What one can never do is to claim the right to destroy it.

Allow me to summarize: There is a moral difference between

killing and allowing to die. All killing of patients is morally wrong while allowing some patients to die is not. The moral evaluation of these acts is based upon intention. Belief in this distinction allows a middle course between suicide and euthanasia on the one hand, and lingering on a ventilator on the other. Patients need not be overmastered by technology, and can stop treatments that are ineffective or excessively burdensome. But neither do they need to be overmastered by the despair, hopelessness and fear that lead some to kill themselves or to ask to be killed.

Euthanasia is not death with dignity, nor is dying alone with a plastic bag over one's head, spitting up the pills one has tried to force down one's own throat. Killing is the ultimate indignity. To be allowed to die in the company of loved ones, reminded that as one passes away into the mystery of death, one's life has meaning and value in the eyes of God, family and community, even in the face of dependency and pain, is real death with dignity. Killing and allowing to die are not the same.

| "As Catholics we believe euthanasia
is morally wrong because it is the
destruction of life."

EUTHANASIA VIOLATES CHRISTIAN BELIEFS

Michigan Catholic Conference

In the following viewpoint, the members of the Michigan Catholic Conference argue that euthanasia is a violation of the biblical prohibition against killing. The authors believe that how a person chooses to die can either inspire others or send a message that some lives are burdensome and without value. In the authors' view, all persons, because they have been created by God, have a dignity that is not diminished by their suffering or dependence on others. Truly compassionate persons, claim the authors, seek to eliminate suffering but never to eliminate the sufferer. The Michigan Catholic Conference serves as the coordinating unit for the Catholic Church in Michigan and issues public policy statements on its behalf.

As you read, consider the following questions:

1. What is the Church's position on aggressive and burdensome medical treatments, as described by the authors?
2. How does the Church's concept of "dignity" contrast with society's definition of the term, according to the members of the Michigan Catholic Conference?
3. In the authors' words, what are the two voices in the euthanasia debate?

Excerpted from the letter "Living and Dying According to the Voice of Faith: A Pastoral Letter to the Catholics of the State of Michigan," by the Michigan Catholic Conference, 1997, by permission of the Michigan Catholic Conference.

W̲e, the Bishops of the seven Dioceses of Michigan, are taking the unprecedented step of writing this joint Pastoral Letter to share with you our Catholic convictions on assisted suicide and the meaning of genuine compassion. We take this extraordinary step because there is so much confusion and anxiety on moral questions surrounding dying and death. These critical questions call for a decisive response—from us as shepherds, from our whole Catholic community, and from all who share our respect for the dignity of human life.

In recent years, our Great Lakes State has acquired a dubious distinction as a high-profile, publicity-driven laboratory for assisted suicide. Current legislative and initiative efforts are seeking to legalize assisted suicide for vulnerable patients. It is from our pastoral concern that we seek to help Catholics form their consciences at this critical time. . . .

DYING IS PART OF LIVING

We often think that death is the end of the story. We forget that it is foreshadowed throughout our life; dying is woven into the very fiber of our life from its inception. The voice of faith reassures us that we need not fear death but at the same time, because we are human, we can still be anxious about the circumstances of our death. Not knowing what the future may hold, we do not want to give up all the opportunities and gifts around us. When it is time for us to leave this world, it is fitting that we should want to die in a way that is meaningful, even beautiful and inspiring—for us and for all those we love.

In the dying process, there is still a great scope for personal choice and responsibility: How we face the mysteries of suffering, dying, and death makes a critical difference for us and for our loved ones who wish to offer us compassionate support. As stewards of the gift of life, we see every aspect of life and death as part of a larger picture and part of our ongoing relationship with God and neighbor.

Choosing death by one's own hand contradicts our deepest identity as sons and daughters of God. Such an action also conveys a tragic message to our family and friends—that we reject their genuine love and our solidarity with them.

CHOOSING LIFE

Suicide—the conscious choice to destroy one's own life—is always morally wrong. Concurring with someone's intention to commit suicide and cooperating in the process can never be condoned. Such assisted suicide is a perversion of genuine mercy. It is especially tragic when undertaken by physicians whose very professional code charges them never to harm but always to respect life.

For several years there has been a continuing debate about the legality—and practice—of assisted suicide in Michigan. On the national scene, the United States Supreme Court upheld laws banning assisted suicide in the states of Washington and New York and said there is no constitutional right to assisted suicide. We need such a statutory ban in our own state: to protect the vulnerable, to prevent unscrupulous and unethical medical practices, to guarantee the best possible care for all, and to affirm the value of human life.

Above and beyond what civil laws may say, we Christians are ultimately responsible to God our Creator. As a Church, we definitively say "no" to assisted suicide because we say "yes" to life—from the first moment of conception until our last natural breath. Suicide in any form prevents us from fulfilling the plan God intended for us when we were given life.

Euthanasia, or so called "mercy killing," may at first sound like an appealing form of death because it proposes to eliminate all suffering. Yet it is not at all what it seems! By definition, euthanasia is any action that of itself and by intention causes death so as to relieve suffering. As Catholics we believe euthanasia is morally wrong because it is the destruction of life. It also opens the door to other potential crimes against life, especially against those who are chronically ill or disabled. Euthanasia is unnecessary as well as wrong because suffering and pain can be relieved in many morally acceptable ways.

THE CHURCH'S RESPECT FOR PAIN MANAGEMENT

Our Ethical and Religious Directives for Catholic Health Care Services state that, "Dying patients who request euthanasia should receive loving care, psychological and spiritual support, and appropriate remedies for pain and other symptoms so that they can live with dignity until the time of natural death."

As Catholics we recognize that life is not an absolute which must be preserved at all costs. We are not required to continue life in each and every circumstance.

Dying patients and their caregivers have the right and responsibility to determine whether a particular means of treatment is necessary. If, in consultation with their physician, they rightly judge a treatment to be useless or unduly burdensome, patients are free to undergo the treatment or to forgo it. When death is clearly inevitable and close at hand, a patient or caregiver can make the decision to forgo aggressive medical treatment which would impose an excessive burden on patient and family. In such cases, the Church particularly encourages pain management and hospice care for the dying. Further, patients and their caregivers have a legitimate right to insist on the best and most effective pain management and treatment to minimize suffering. One may even legitimately choose to relieve pain by use of medications which may have the unfortunate side effect of decreasing consciousness or shortening one's life, if this is done with the intent of relieving pain, and no other means are available to serve this goal. This is very different from the direct intention to take life, as in euthanasia. . . .

LIVING AND DYING ARE INTERWOVEN

No human being has absolute control over his or her own life; God alone has dominion over all creation. Since many aspects of life exceed our immediate control, we have to learn to accept gracefully the limitations imposed by time and circumstances, relationships and commitments, economic realities and other factors. We find peace of mind and heart precisely when we come to terms with the fact that life is a mystery, a gift from God, a blessing over which we do not have complete control.

We are born into a social network, a family of one kind or another, and various communities. Our life story is interwoven with those of our families and communities; we are accountable to them as well as to God. Our individual identity and rights do not separate us from others but should call us into greater communion and solidarity with them.

Every right brings with it responsibilities for the good of all. Our decisions about life and death are never purely private matters, for many other persons are necessarily involved—doctors, nurses, family and friends. Our choices in dying have a profound impact on those we leave behind. They also influence others who are suffering in body or spirit, especially the elderly, the dying, the chronically ill, and persons who are physically or mentally challenged. By the way we live and die we can inspire and console them—or we can add to the voices that tell them their lives are burdensome and without value. . . .

TRUE COMPASSION FOR THE DYING

Euthanasia may be seen as the "dark side" of our conviction that medicine should solve all our health problems. If we cannot cure the dying, we are tempted to say that the "next best thing" may be the "compassionate" step of eliminating their very lives.

This is not a healthy understanding of the role of the healing profession. Nor does it reflect authentic compassion.

Compassion literally means "to suffer with," to share patiently in the experience of someone else's pain—be it psychological stress or physical trauma. In the Biblical language, compassion has to do with the heart or womb. The heart is moved to love because the heart senses its solidarity with the one in need. Compassion also has to do with the womb; in the depths of our being we make space for the other. True compassion does not eliminate the sufferer but seeks to relieve the suffering. While medicine cannot solve every problem, it can help us to provide patients with the best possible support and comfort.

FALSE MERCY

To concur with the intention of another person to commit suicide and to help in carrying it out through so-called "assisted suicide" means to cooperate in, and at times to be the actual perpetrator of, an injustice which can never be excused, even if it is requested. In a remarkably relevant passage Saint Augustine writes that "it is never licit to kill another: even if he should wish it, indeed if he request it because, hanging between life and death, he begs for help in freeing the soul struggling against the bonds of the body and longing to be released; nor is it licit even when a sick person is no longer able to live".

Even when not motivated by a selfish refusal to be burdened with the life of someone who is suffering, euthanasia must be called a *false mercy*, and indeed a disturbing "perversion" of mercy. True "compassion" leads to sharing another's pain; it does not kill the person whose suffering we cannot bear. Moreover, the act of euthanasia appears all the more perverse if it is carried out by those, like relatives, who are supposed to treat a family member with patience and love, or by those, such as doctors, who by virtue of their specific profession are supposed to care for the sick person even in the most painful terminal stages.

John Paul II, *Evangelium Vitae (On the Value and Inviolability of Human Life)*, March 25, 1995.

Having shared in the experiences of many dying people and their families, Dr. Ira Byock, President of the American Academy of Hospice and Palliative Medicine, has listed the "five last things" which people most want or need at the end of their lives: granting forgiveness, seeking forgiveness, expressing gratitude, demonstrating love, and saying good-bye. The compassionate presence of family and friends sanctifies the dying process by allowing these steps to occur among loving, supportive people.

Understanding "Dignity" and "Death with Dignity"

Our technological society sometimes seems to tell us that our dignity comes from being useful. At the very least, we must be able to take care of ourselves. Yet our own Declaration of Independence teaches us that our dignity comes from having been created by God with unalienable rights. Our Christian faith says something much more: we have value and dignity simply because we are God's children, and we have been redeemed by the Death-Resurrection of Jesus. These are permanent gifts which death cannot destroy.

Even when we are dependent on medical staff, family and friends, we still have much to give to others. Silently but dramatically, dying persons remind us of our ultimate human vocation and destiny; in their absolute dependence, they teach us that being matters more than doing.

Facing our inevitable death, we recognize our ultimate solidarity with every other person. Dying and death are not the final separation from others, but rather something all human beings have in common. No matter what other differences may separate us, in dying we enter into the fullness of human solidarity.

The late Joseph Cardinal Bernardin of Chicago offered us an eloquent example of how life and death are connected. By the way he freely embraced the prospect of approaching death, he taught us that the way we die is very significant, even a source of potential blessing and peace—for ourselves and for others. Instead of thinking of death as enemy, he came to see it as friend. Handing himself over to the process of dying from cancer, he allowed his own life story to be immersed in the Death and Resurrection of Jesus.

Overcoming Fear with Faith

The voice of faith challenges us to form our conscience by standards which transcend the values around us. Hearing our daily news in "sound bites" and feeling overwhelmed by the complexity of issues and the pace of events, we can look for expedient ways of solving problems, losing sight of the necessary steps of conscience formation: prayer, reflection, and dialogue. . . .

In our haste and under pressure, we can easily make the mistake of identifying what is "legal" with what is "moral." They are not always the same! There are times when our state and federal legislation fall short of a moral standard which upholds the value and dignity of human life. The authority of all earthly governments is limited; first and foremost, we are under God's law.

Our Christian consciences compel us to act in accord with

God's will, with His plan for our well-being. In the depths of our hearts, the voice of God reiterates the same ageless message: "Thou shalt not kill." So it is that we must take the time to form our consciences rather than "going with the flow" of what is apparently convenient or popular.

Right now, throughout our state, two contrasting voices vie for our attention and seek to win our allegiance.

The Voice of Fear says:

Zealously guard control of your own life and destiny; you can keep ultimate control by choosing when to take your life.

Look out for what is most expedient for yourself; let others take care of themselves as they can.

Exit this world while you are still at your best; otherwise people resent you for being a burden.

The Voice of Faith says:

My life is a great blessing and gift; I trust that God who gave it to me will not desert me.

I am a part of a great family of humanity; how I choose to live and die influences the life and destiny of my brothers and sisters.

I will enter the dying process with all its mysteries with trust in God and in solidarity with my brothers and sisters; I will die with the dignity of letting myself be loved unconditionally.

We urge you to listen to the voice of faith. Pray over our message and consider its application in your own life. Discuss it with your families and friends and in your parishes. Let this voice of faith take root in your heart so it may influence all that you do and say, especially how you view dying and death. . . .

We are at a defining moment for our State of Michigan. Our situation challenges us to remain true to the values of life and faith. May we live according to the voice of faith!

"I see the holiness of life enhanced, not
diminished, by letting people have a
say in how they choose to die."

EUTHANASIA DOES NOT VIOLATE
CHRISTIAN BELIEFS

John Shelby Spong

In the following viewpoint, John Shelby Spong argues that assisted suicide may sometimes be morally acceptable to Christians. Spong asserts that modern medicine has an incredible
ability to prolong life, but he contends that some treatments can
destroy a person's ability to relate to others, making their last
days meaningless. In Spong's view, these complex situations
compel Christians to reevaluate their views on assisted suicide.
He believes assisted suicide should be an individual choice and
that neither the government nor the church should condemn it.
Spong is an Episcopalian bishop and the author of *Why Christianity Must Change or Die* and *Rescuing the Bible from Fundamentalism: A Bishop
Rethinks the Meaning of Scripture.*

As you read, consider the following questions:

1. How have advances in medicine affected the traditional
   distinction between active and passive euthanasia, according
   to Spong?
2. In the author's words, what must life "not be identified
   with"?
3. What right does the author describe as "a peculiar gift of this
   modern world"?

Reprinted from John Shelby Spong's testimony before the U.S. House of Representatives
Committee on the Judiciary, Subcommittee on the Constitution, April 29, 1996.

There are two enormous pitfalls that stand ready to make the national debate on assisted suicide deeply emotional and highly partisan.

The first lies in the traditional definition of the word "suicide" which brings to mind an act of self-destruction associated with depression and mental illness. Religious voices through the ages have called this suicide unnatural and sinful, going so far as to refuse to perform burial services for suicide victims. The religious and political rhetoric reflecting these attitudes of the past now threatens to distort the present debate with inappropriate hyperbole.

The second pitfall appears when assisted suicide becomes a pawn in the abortion debate. The connector is usually found in some aspect of the phrase "the right to life." The morality of abortion is a worthy debate on which good and decent people hold deeply contrasting views, but to confuse assisted suicide with abortion is both inappropriate and misleading.

In assisted suicide the choice to end one's life under certain circumstances takes place at the end of the life cycle, and it is a choice made by the affected person. Abortion occurs when the life of the fetus is still potential, and is an action in which the subject is neither consulted nor given a choice. Assisted suicide and abortion are thus quite different.

PROLONGING LIFE VERSUS POSTPONING DEATH

The concept of assisted suicide is a peculiarly modern topic. It was all but inconceivable a century ago. It is before us today because of human ingenuity. Advances in the practice of medicine and the spectacular development of various medical technologies are the co-parents of this debate. Medical science has succeeded in so many areas. Pain is today capable of being relieved in remarkably effective ways. Many killing diseases have been conquered. Both the boundaries and the quality of life have been extended beyond anything our ancestors could have imagined.

These are remarkable achievements in which we can rightfully rejoice. But, this very success has created for us the dilemmas out of which the assisted suicide debate has arisen. For it is the skill of medical science that has enabled us to cross that mysterious boundary that separates the prolonging of life and good health from the ability simply to postpone death. We must recognize this subtle distinction. To enhance the length and beauty of life is clearly a value, but simply to prevent death is at best a questionable virtue.

We human beings now have arrived at a set of circumstances

that requires us to embrace the freedom and to find the courage to decide for ourselves how long our life will be extended and under what circumstances our deaths shall occur.

MEDICAL ADVANCES CONFOUND TRADITIONAL RELIGIOUS TEACHINGS

Once there was a neat distinction between what religious people called passive and active euthanasia. Passive euthanasia meant the refusal to take extraordinary means to extend life and it was generally approved by traditional religious teaching. Active euthanasia meant taking an overt action to hasten death and it was generally condemned by traditional religious thinking. That distinction, however, has been rendered all but meaningless by the advances in modern medicine.

Today, decisions by doctors and family members to remove or not to remove life support systems and to assist nature or to let nature take its course are daily occurrences in hospitals across this nation. That spectre causes many people to seek the assurance that the patient will have some say about his or her destiny prior to that moment of life. Many of us want the moral and legal right to choose to die with our faculties intact, surrounded by those we love before we are reduced to being breathing cadavers, attended by strangers, with no human dignity attached to our final days.

We are aware that life can today be prolonged by managing pain with pain-killing drugs, but that relief is sometimes achieved at the price of the destruction of the patient's mind or the loss of the patient's capacity to relate to other human beings in a meaningful way. Surely the prolongation of a person's days in a meaningless breathing body is not a witness to the sacredness of life.

These are the situations out of which the demand arises for some legal means to preserve the individual's right to make an informed decision about the way he or she will die. Surely the right to make so personal a decision as this should not be abrogated by the state, nor should it be condemned by any part of the Christian Church. The legal right to die with dignity is an essential new modern freedom from which mature human beings dare not shrink. Life must not be identified with the extension of biological existence.

ABUSES ARE POSSIBLE BUT NOT INEVITABLE

Another factor in this decision-making process arises from the incredible expense of terminal care. Obviously the value of life cannot be measured in economic terms alone, and economic considerations must never drive this debate. Yet, when the options are clear and a patient knows that he or she faces days, weeks, perhaps even a few months of expensive, pain-filled, not always conscious life with no hope of long-range cure, then at least I, as one citizen, want to be given the right, morally and legally, to make a decision for myself. I want the ability to weigh the value of those additional days, weeks, or even months of my existence against the costs that my family would have to pay, both in terms of their financial resources and their emotional reserves. Because of the love I have for my wife and my children, I want to be able to cast my vote for what is in their best interest, even if that means choosing the quicker end rather than allowing the inevitable lingering dissipation of my mind and body.

If leaders of religious and political organizations want to look

---

A Jewish View of Euthanasia

Jewish tradition puts a high premium on extending life but recognizes that prolonging the process of painful death is not necessarily desirable. Therefore, the tradition endorses *passive euthanasia* in most cases where death is imminent and inevitable and where the process of dying is accompanied by unbearable anguish. This attitude also relates to the introduction of heroic measures. When death is near and certain and where considerable pain will ensue, such measures are not encouraged; indeed, according to some authorities, they are proscribed.

The dominant view in Jewish sources prohibits *active euthanasia* of any kind. However, in view of contemporary realities I have felt it necessary to defend, within the framework of classical Jewish sources, a position that would justify active euthanasia in certain circumstances. I believe that in the case of terminally ill persons with no hope of recovery, with irreparable vital-organ damage, who have exhausted all medical remedies, and whose last days are overwhelmed with unbearable agony, the patients, their families, physicians, health-care workers, and social-service professionals should be able to advocate and to practice active euthanasia without feeling that they have transgressed divine and human laws, without being burdened with great guilt for actions that they sincerely consider merciful.

To be sure, Judaism instructs us to "choose life" (Deut. 30:19). But Judaism also recognizes that "there is a time to die" (Eccles. 3:2). Whenever the problem of euthanasia presents itself, each person involved must decide which verse applies and how the principle therein may best be implemented.

Byron L. Sherwin, *In Partnership with God: Contemporary Jewish Law and Ethics*, 1990.

---

at the immorality of applying an economic agenda to the present debate, I suggest that their focus should not be on the issue of assisted suicide. Rather, we should look at the rich capital gains being accrued to smart investors in health care industries and at those million-dollar bonuses paid to CEOs of HMOs. The failure of this nation to enact universal health care has also consigned the bottom 20 percent of our population to grossly inadequate medical attention that dooms many to an involuntary early death. Surely immorality also resides there.

Of course, there are dangers when a society decides to allow its citizens this freedom of choice at the end of life. Convenience and greed, in cooperation with a few unscrupulous members of the medical profession, have the potential to create a world of horrors for many people. Those dangers, however, are not inevitable.

I suppose it will be quite impossible for all malfeasance to be eliminated from this area of life. Malfeasance has not been eliminated completely from any other area of human activity. I do suggest, however, that this is only an excuse, and a poor one at that, when we assume that the same human brilliance that has produced the miracle of modern medicine cannot also solve the problem of prohibiting improper decisions while still allowing individuals the choice of how they want to live out their final days.

When human beings have done an audacious thing, we ought not to tremble before the choices presented to us by our own audacity. Safeguards can be put into place. The slippery slope arguments against assisted suicide, continually offered by those who seem to fear every new possibility, can be addressed.

ASSISTED SUICIDE IS CONSISTENT WITH CHRISTIAN ETHICS AND AMERICAN VALUES

Finally, I want to be clear, particularly because the common wisdom is that religious voices are overwhelmingly opposed to assisted suicide, that I have come to these conclusions as a Christian and out of my Judeo-Christian faith tradition. I state them to the world and to the Church at large specifically as an Episcopal Bishop. My personal creed asserts that every person is sacred, created in God's image; that every person is loved by God in Jesus Christ, and that every person is called into the fullness of his or her humanity by the Holy Spirit. I see the holiness of life enhanced, not diminished, by letting people have a say in how they choose to die.

I also believe that we live in a country which endows its citizens with certain inalienable rights. Among those rights, newly given, as a peculiar gift of this modern world, is the right to participate in the management of our own deaths.

Assisted suicide must never be a requirement, but it should always be a legal and moral option. This decision to end one's life needs to be faced openly, honestly, freely and in consultation with our loved ones, our doctors, and our spiritual advisors. When the decision on assisted suicide is made this way, I am convinced that it is a life-affirming moral choice. It is also a human right that I hope this Congress will grant to the American people.

| "The problem of aiding people who
face prolonged dying is so great that
we cannot ignore it."

VOLUNTARY EUTHANASIA SHOWS COMPASSION FOR THE DYING

Marcia Angell

In the following viewpoint, Marcia Angell, executive editor of the *New England Journal of Medicine*, argues that in some cases compassion requires doctors to respect a dying patient's request for euthanasia or assisted suicide. Angell contrasts voluntary euthanasia, assisted suicide, and the removal of life-sustaining treatment, and contends that voluntary euthanasia is often the most humane of these options because it allows a doctor, at the patient's request, to administer a fast, painless death. In the author's opinion, removal of treatment alone is an inadequate response to the needs of dying patients because it does not address their suffering.

As you read, consider the following questions:

1. In Angell's opinion, what are the traditional moral distinctions between voluntary euthanasia, assisted suicide, and removal of treatment based on, and why does she find these distinctions unpersuasive?
2. What does the author say is the most frequently heard argument against permitting assisted suicide?
3. What does the author believe are the best forms of assisted dying if the goal is to a) maximize the self-determination of the patient and b) minimize the patient's suffering?

Excerpted from Marcia Angell, "Helping Desperately Ill People to Die," in Linda L. Emanuel, ed., *Regulating How We Die: The Ethical, Medical, and Legal Issues Surrounding Physician-Assisted Suicide* (Cambridge, Mass: Harvard University Press). Reprinted by permission of the publisher. Copyright ©1998 by the President and Fellows of Harvard College.

In [the late 1960s], physicians and their instructors paid little formal attention to the dying process. I do not remember a single mention of it in the medical school curriculum. It was as though dying were a medical failure and thus too shameful to be discussed. We were to succeed, not fail. When we came up against the reality of dying patients and their suffering, as I did in my internship, we were largely on our own. If patients asked for help in dying, they might or might not receive it. Whether they did depended more on us—our compassion, courage, and ingenuity—than it did on the patient's condition. In most cases, a patient's death was hastened without an explicit request by the patient or the family, although often there was an implicit understanding. For example, patients would say that they would rather be dead than continue pointless suffering, and families would ask the doctor whether "something" could be done. A doctor at that point might stop antibiotics or transfusions or whatever life-sustaining treatment was being given, often adding large doses of morphine as well.

Many doctors thought it was wrong to stop life-saving treatment, however, even if the patient requested it. They believed that their job was to extend life whenever possible. In those days, little distinction was made among the various methods of shortening life. All were forbidden. Most doctors also had an exaggerated fear of the addictive properties and side-effects of morphine. Furthermore, medical practice was highly paternalistic. Doctors rarely spoke with patients about decisions at the end of life; they simply made them. Seeking explicit agreement to hasten death would have been seen as unkind, as well as incriminating and unnecessary. In any case, the matter was far removed from public discussion, much less a subject of political controversy. What happened in any given case was at the doctor's discretion. It was all very private, and no policies or procedures governed the situation.

THE RIGHT TO REFUSE TREATMENT

Enormous changes have occurred since then. For one thing, the consumer movement, fostered by the legal doctrine of informed consent, has greatly limited the ability of doctors to act alone. So, too, has the development of a team approach to hospital care. Increasingly, decisions must be discussed not only with patients but among all members of the health care team. More important, the issue became a public matter in 1975, when Joseph Quinlan went to court to ask for the authority to discontinue all "extraordinary procedures" keeping his daughter, Karen Ann, alive. Suddenly the "right to die" was not just a private matter but a legal, ethical, and social issue.

Other legal cases followed the Quinlan case. As these poignant stories were publicized, large numbers of healthy people for the first time began to think about whether extending life might produce more suffering than benefit. They became aware that modern medicine was a two-edged sword, capable of dramatically rescuing some people from death, while damning others to prolonged suffering. Beginning in 1976, the state legislatures, one by one, enacted Natural Death Acts, which gave doctors immunity from prosecution if, under certain circumstances, they complied with a patient's living will and withheld or withdrew life-sustaining treatment. President Reagan established a Commission for the Study of Ethical Problems in Medicine, which in 1983 issued its report, *Deciding to Forgo Life-Sustaining Treatment.* In it, the Commission laid out principled procedures for approaching the problem of suffering at the end of life. These supported the concept of withholding life-sustaining treatment under defined circumstances. Physician-assisted dying had become a public issue, and doctors could no longer act alone on a case-by-case basis.

MORAL DISTINCTIONS

With increasing attention to the manner of dying came explicit distinctions that had not always been recognized. Withholding life-sustaining treatment, such as an artificial respirator, dialysis, or antibiotics, was held to be morally different from assisting in suicide by writing a prescription for large amounts of barbiturates, for example. And both of these acts were different from euthanasia, that is, actively causing death by giving a lethal injection. It became generally accepted that withholding life-sustaining treatment was permissible, but euthanasia was not. Assisting suicide—making it possible for a patient to take his own life—remains more contentious. It is thought by some to be appropriate under certain circumstances, but many believe it is always wrong. The ambiguous position of assisted suicide is mirrored in the law. Suicide is not illegal, but in most, though not all states, assisting in suicide is.

The purpose of all three acts—withholding life-sustaining treatment, assisting suicide, and euthanasia—is the same: to hasten death. They are often thought of as constituting a continuum from passive to active. To withhold life-sustaining treatment simply means to refrain from initiating a treatment or to withdraw a treatment that has already been initiated. Thus, not placing a patient on an artificial respirator would be passive, even though it resulted in death, as would removing a respirator from a patient already using it. Writing a prescription for an overdose is seen as more active. Even though it is up to the patient to actually take the overdose, the doctor has actively supplied the means. Euthanasia is the most active, in that death is caused by an explicit act.

CONFUSING ELEMENTS

Paradoxically, however, from the patient's perspective, euthanasia is probably the most humane of the three events, since it is fast and painless. Withholding life-sustaining treatment may be much less humane, in that it extends the dying process and accentuates symptoms (such as suffocation or fever) until death occurs. Despite the differing moral status of the three methods of shortening life, it is often difficult to appreciate the differences in practical terms. For example, withdrawing a respirator requires removing the machine and a period of agonal struggle for breath as the patient dies. This is not a "passive" scene—it is stressful for the patient, for attending physicians and nurses, and for family members at the bedside. Furthermore, if it occurred against the wishes of the patient, it would constitute murder. By contrast, injecting an overdose of morphine into an intravenous line produces a quiet, peaceful death, even though doing so constitutes "active" euthanasia.

There is another confusing element. Both withdrawing treatment and euthanasia do not require the participation of the patient. Either could be done without the patient's cooperation. In contrast, assisted suicide—the morally "intermediate" act—*does* require the patient's participation. To die, the patient must swallow the pills—a voluntary act of a necessarily aware patient. Thus, the traditional moral distinctions are entirely based on what the doctor does, not on the consequences of the doctor's action for the patient. The question asked is the nature of the doctor's act: Is it passive or active or intermediate? The moral judgment is divorced from the patient's perspective. We do not usually ask how the patient is affected. Because the patient seems left out of the moral equation, the distinctions seem to me somewhat artificial and ultimately unpersuasive.

ASSISTED SUICIDE IN THE COURTS

Until [the late 1980s], none of the methods of hastening death was generally accepted. Now, withholding life-sustaining treatment is not only accepted but commonplace. The controversy is about more active means of hastening death. . . .

In 1996 two federal appeals courts took the matter out of the hands of the state legislatures in their jurisdictions. The U.S. Court of Appeals for the Ninth Circuit declared unconstitutional Washington's law against physician-assisted suicide. A month later, the Court of Appeals for the Second Circuit declared unconstitutional a similar law in New York. Both were reversed by the U.S. Supreme Court. The Ninth Circuit Court had invoked the due process clause of the Fourteenth Amendment; the Second Circuit based its decision on the equal protection clause. But both courts found no moral distinction between assisted suicide and withholding life-sustaining treatment. Many believe that, quite apart from the merits of the arguments, the courts were arrogating to themselves decisions that properly belonged to the legislatures. Others believe that since decisions at the end of life are essentially private decisions involving individual rights, the courts are the proper forum.

FEAR OF THE SLIPPERY SLOPE

The most frequent argument against permitting assisted suicide is that it would inevitably lead to a gradual erosion of our respect for life. According to this view, there is no landmark on this slippery moral slope to tell us we've gone too far and no purchase to stop the slide. I find this argument unpersuasive in the abstract. Life is full of slippery slopes, and one of our more interesting duties is negotiating them. If we stayed off them altogether, we could accomplish very little.

But the argument is much more persuasive in the particular case of the United States at the end of this century. Unlike the situation in other Western democracies, caring for a family member with a long illness in the United States can be financially devastating. And we do little as a society to help with the other difficulties of caring for the chronically ill. Given the heavy burdens, then, mightn't there be pressures on sick people with expensive illnesses to ask to die? And wouldn't this pressure be greatest among the very old, the poor, and the handicapped—who may be too weak to resist the pressure? And in this social context, with all its economic harshness, mightn't voluntary euthanasia, requested by the patient, be extended to involuntary euthanasia of incompetent patients, first for their own sakes, then for the sake of their families, then for the budget of the health care system? These are the practical slippery-slope concerns that I have. They do not apply with nearly the same force to a country such as the Netherlands, where there is a universal and comprehensive health care system and where a lingering illness does not bankrupt the family.

Despite these concerns, it seems to me that the problem of aiding people who face prolonged dying is so great that we cannot ignore it. Any of us may be in the situation some day, and it behooves all of us to develop our thinking on the matter. We cannot avoid the slippery slope; in fact, with the growing acceptance since Quinlan of the right to withhold life-sustaining treatment, we are already on it, like it or not. The issue now is simply where and how to find a purchase. The 1996 decision of the Ninth Circuit Court of Appeals declaring unconstitutional Washington's law against physician-assisted suicide emphasized this point.

I believe there are two alternative ways we might deal with the problem, while preventing a headlong slide downhill. The first is to permit physician-assisted suicide under certain circumstances, but not euthanasia. By definition, suicide requires the patient to act; euthanasia does not. By limiting assisted dying to suicide, patients retain ultimate control and they can change their minds at any time, as was emphasized by the Second Circuit Court of Appeals. To be sure, an occasional, ambivalent patient may succumb to outside pressures, but no system of safeguards for any workable endeavor is absolutely foolproof. The crucial point is that, unlike either euthanasia or withholding life-sustaining treatment, suicide requires a deliberate action by the patient.

An alternative way to negotiate the slippery slope would be to draw the line strictly between voluntary and involuntary euthanasia. Euthanasia would be permitted, but only for competent patients who request it, as in the Netherlands. Unlike assisted suicide, it would not exclude patients who, because of their illness, cannot swallow pills. It would, however, exclude patients who are not competent, and it would also exclude children, as well as adults with advanced Alzheimer's disease. But perhaps these limitations are the price of preventing abuse. Indeed, euthanasia so restricted might be a second stage in legalizing physician-assisted dying, to be considered only after we as a society, perhaps in only a few states, have had some experience with legally sanctioned physician-assisted suicide.

Dying in Agony

Whatever our approach, the problem of dying in agony will not go away. In my view, it is time to incorporate physician-assisted suicide into our medical armamentarium, to be used infrequently under certain well-defined circumstances. It should be available for those facing slow disintegration, and for those overwhelmed by the infirmities of old age, as well as for those in the throes of advanced disease. As in the Dutch guidelines, it should not be used as an answer to depression or other treatable illness. Modern medicine now performs great miracles, but it also produces great anguish, not all of which can be relieved even by the most assiduous attempts to treat pain.

SELF-DETERMINATION AND MERCY

The moral argument in favor of permitting physician assistance in suicide is grounded in the conjunction of two principles: self-determination (or, as bioethicists put it, autonomy) and mercy (or the avoidance of suffering). The moral right of self-determination is the right to live one's life as one sees fit, subject only to the constraint that this not involve harm to others. Because living one's life as one chooses must also include living the very end of one's life as one chooses, the matter of how to die is as fully protected by the principle of self-determination as any other part of one's life. Choosing how to die is part of choosing how to live.

The second component of the moral argument in favor of physician assistance in suicide is grounded in the joint obligations to avoid doing harm and to do good (the principles of nonmaleficence and beneficence, as bioethicists often put them). In medical-ethics discussions, some writers call this the principle of patient interests or patient welfare, but in the specific context of end-of-life questions, I like to call this the principle of mercy— the principle that one ought both to refrain from causing pain or suffering and act to relieve it. The principle of mercy, or avoidance of suffering, underwrites the right of a dying person to an easy death, to whatever extent possible, and clearly supports physician-assisted suicide in many cases. Suicide assisted by a humane physician spares the patient the pain and suffering that may be part of the dying process, and grants the patient a "mercifully" easy death.

Margaret P. Battin, "Is a Physician Ever Obligated to Help a Patient Die?" in Linda L. Emanuel, ed., *Regulating How We Die*, 1998.

Polls of doctors indicate that a majority of them, like the public at large, believe assisted suicide or euthanasia is sometimes appropriate. But among these doctors, about half believe that the act should be performed by someone else, not a doctor. They believe that a doctor's function must be to extend life, never to shorten it. To them, an absolute proscription against physician-assisted dying prevents confusion on the part of doctors and distrust on the part of patients. Doctors need never wonder whether they should be extending life or cutting it short, and patients need never wonder what their doctor is up to. I find this position peculiarly divorced from the real business of medicine—to provide care in whatever way best serves the patient's interests. If acceding to a patient's request to hasten death seems appropriate to the doctor, how can he or she justify withdrawing from the patient's care at that point? The greatest harm we can do is to abandon a desperate patient.

THE PATIENT'S PERSPECTIVE

Most of the arguments against physician-assisted suicide place the doctor at the center of the issue. Is the doctor's act one of omission or commission? Is it consistent with the doctor's role? If this is the focus, it is reasonable to argue that withholding life-sustaining treatment is permissible but not assisted suicide or euthanasia. If we shift the focus from the doctor to the patient, however, the calculus changes. Suppose instead of asking about the doctor's act, we ask whether the *patient's* act is one of omission or commission—that is, is the patient required to perform the final action or can it be done by someone else, perhaps without the patient's full knowledge or consent? If we wish to maximize self-determination for the patient, assisted suicide is more reasonable than either euthanasia or merely withholding treatment.

A second question would be whether the patient's death will be as quick and painless as possible or whether there will still be a period of suffering. If degree of suffering is the standard, then euthanasia is probably the best form of assisted dying. The point is that by placing the patient, not the doctor, in the center of the picture, we may come to very different conclusions about the moral status of the ways doctors might help suffering patients to die.

OTHER POSITIVE EFFECTS

Permitting physician-assisted suicide might have positive effects in addition to minimizing suffering. Some patients facing an irreversible progressive disease take their own lives while they are still in reasonably good health, because they fear that if they wait, they will find themselves unable to do so—either because they are too impaired to act or because they are confined to a hospital. Knowing that assisted death would be available when they needed it would undoubtedly lead many incurably ill people to postpone ending their lives. They would thus live longer and, even more important, they would live in more peace.

This effect was clear in Dr. Timothy E. Quill's account of his patient, Diane. Once she had the prescription for a lethal dose of sleeping pills, her anxiety subsided and she was able to enjoy wholeheartedly her remaining months with her family. The same phenomenon was described in a 1995 article in *The New Yorker* by Andrew Solomon. Solomon recounted the story of his mother's death from ovarian cancer. Only after she stockpiled enough sleeping pills to kill herself was she able to achieve some measure of happiness in the time remaining to her.

The problems of prolonged dying are not new, but they have become more urgent in recent years because we now have the technology to extend life long after some people would wish to be dead. There is little precedent for the kinds of decisions we need to make. Merely having the right to refuse life-sustaining treatment does not solve the problem of prolonged dying for all patients. We need to do more for them. To be sure, we must choose our way carefully, mindful of the possibilities of abuse. But paralysis is not an answer, and moralism is no substitute for compassion.

| "Euthanasia is not about the right to
| die. It's about the right to kill."

ARGUMENTS FOR EUTHANASIA ARE UNCONVINCING

International Anti-Euthanasia Task Force

The International Anti-Euthanasia Task Force (IAETF) is an advocacy group based in Steubenville, Ohio, that opposes the legalization of euthanasia and assisted suicide. In the following viewpoint, the IAETF responds to several popular arguments for euthanasia, arguing that euthanasia advocates use euphemisms and false claims to support their beliefs. For example, write the authors, dying patients have the right to refuse treatment, so the claim that doctors might force a patient to stay alive is unfounded. In the IAETF's view, killing is always wrong—requests for euthanasia stem from pain and depression, and both of these problems can be treated.

As you read, consider the following questions:

1. How do the authors define euthanasia?
2. What is the purpose of laws against euthanasia, in the authors' opinion?
3. What euphemisms do euthanasia advocates use to disguise the fact that euthanasia is killing, according to the IAETF?

Reprinted from "Euthanasia: Answers to Frequently Asked Questions," by the International Anti-Euthanasia Task Force, at www.iaetf.org/faq.htm, by permission of the International Anti-Euthanasia Task Force.

Euthanasia is one of the most important public policy issues being debated today. The outcome of that debate will profoundly affect family relationships, interaction between doctors and patients, and concepts of basic morality. With so much at stake, more is needed than a duel of one-liners, slogans and sound bites.

The following answers to frequently asked questions are designed as starting points for considering the issues. . . .

1. What is euthanasia?

Formerly called "mercy killing," euthanasia means intentionally *making* someone die, rather than allowing that person to die naturally. Put bluntly, euthanasia means killing in the name of compassion.

2. What is the difference between euthanasia and assisted suicide?

In euthanasia, one person does something that directly kills another. For example, a doctor gives a lethal injection to a patient.

In assisted suicide, a non-suicidal person knowingly and intentionally provides the means or acts in some way to help a suicidal person kill himself or herself. For example, a doctor writes a prescription for poison, or someone hooks up a face mask and tubing to a canister of carbon monoxide and then instructs the suicidal person on how to push a lever so that she'll be gassed to death.

For all practical purposes, any distinction between euthanasia and assisted suicide has been abandoned today. Information contained in these answers to frequently asked questions will use the word "euthanasia" for both euthanasia and assisted suicide.

DEATH WITHOUT DIGNITY

3. Doesn't euthanasia insure a dignified death?

"Death with dignity" has become a catchphrase used by euthanasia activists, but there's nothing dignified about the methods they advocate. For example, one euthanasia organization distributes a pamphlet on how to cause suffocation with a plastic bag. Most of Jack Kevorkian's "subjects," as he calls them, have been gassed to death with carbon monoxide and some have had their bodies dumped in vehicles left in parking lots.

4. With legalized euthanasia, wouldn't patients die peacefully, surrounded by their families and doctors, instead of being suffocated by plastic bags or gassed with carbon monoxide as happens now?

No. Campaigners for euthanasia often say that, but it's not true. In the two places where laws were passed to allow euthanasia, it was clear that legalizing euthanasia only legitimizes the use of plastic bags and carbon monoxide to kill vulnerable people.

For example, immediately following the passage of Oregon's Measure 16, those who had said that it would enable people to die peacefully with pills did an immediate about face and admitted that it would permit the types of activities carried out by Jack Kevorkian. They also said that, if pills were used, a plastic bag should also be used to ensure death.

A similar situation occurred in Australia's Northern Territory where proponents of euthanasia painted pictures of a calm, peaceful death with the patient surrounded by loved ones.

When guidelines for the Australian measure (which has now been repealed) were written after its passage, it was acknowledged that carbon monoxide gas would be permitted. It was recommended that, if drugs were used for the euthanasia death, family members should be warned that they may wish to leave the room when the patient is being killed since the death may be very unpleasant to observe. (Lethal injections often cause violent convulsions and muscle spasms.)

A particularly chilling method of ending a patient's life was proposed by Dr. Philip Nitschke, a leading Australian euthanasia activist, when he announced that he had developed a computer program for euthanasia so that doctors could remove themselves from the actual death scene.

DYING PATIENTS ALREADY HAVE THE RIGHT TO REFUSE TREATMENT

5. Doesn't modern technology keep people alive who would have died in the past?

Modern medicine has definitely lengthened life spans. In the early part of this century, pneumonia, appendicitis, diabetes, high blood pressure—even an abscessed tooth—likely meant death, often accompanied by excruciating pain. Women had shorter life expectancies than men since many died in childbirth. Antibiotics, immunizations, surgery and many of today's routine therapies or medications were unknown then.

A lot of people think that the person whose death would be a result of euthanasia or assisted suicide would be someone who doesn't want to be forced to remain alive by being hooked up to machines. But the law already permits patients or their surrogates to direct that such interventions be withheld or withdrawn.

6. Should people be forced to stay alive?

No. And neither the law nor medical ethics requires that "everything be done" to keep a person alive. Insistence, against the patient's wishes, that death be postponed by every means available is contrary to law and practice. It would also be cruel and inhumane.

There comes a time when continued attempts to cure are not compassionate, wise, or medically sound. That's where hospice, including in-home hospice care, can be of such help.

That is the time when all efforts should be placed on making the patient's remaining time comfortable. Then, all interventions should be directed to alleviating pain and other symptoms as well as to the provision of emotional and spiritual support for both the patient and the patient's loved ones.

7. Does the government have the right to make people suffer?

Absolutely not. Likewise, the government should not have the right to give one group of people (e.g., doctors) the right to kill another group of people (e.g., their patients).

Euthanasia activists often claim that laws against euthanasia are government mandated suffering. But this claim would be similar to saying that laws against selling contaminated food are government mandated starvation.

Laws against euthanasia are in place to prevent abuse and to protect people from unscrupulous doctors and others. They are not, and never have been, intended to make anyone suffer.

EUTHANASIA IS ABOUT THE RIGHT TO KILL

8. But shouldn't people have the right to commit suicide?

People do have the power to commit suicide. Suicide and attempted suicide are not criminalized. Each and every year, in the United States alone, there are more suicides than homicides.

Suicide is a tragic, individual act. Euthanasia is not about a private act. It's about letting one person facilitate the death of another. That is a matter of very public concern since it can lead to tremendous abuse, exploitation and erosion of care for the most vulnerable people among us.

Euthanasia is not about giving rights to the person who dies but, instead, is about changing the law and public policy so that doctors, relatives and others can directly and intentionally end another person's life.

This change would not give rights to the person who is killed, but to the person who does the killing. In other words, euthanasia is not about the right to die. It's about the right to kill.

9. Isn't "kill" too strong a word for euthanasia?

No. The word "kill" means "to cause the death of."

In 1989, a group of physicians published a report in the *New England Journal of Medicine* in which they concluded that it would be morally acceptable for doctors to give patients suicide information and a prescription for deadly drugs so they can kill themselves. Dr. Ronald Cranford, one of the authors of the report, publicly acknowledged that this is "the same as killing the patient."

While changes in the law would lead to euthanasia being considered a "medical intervention," the reality would not change—the patient would be killed.

Proponents of euthanasia often use euphemisms like "deliverance," "aid-in-dying" and "gentle landing." If a public policy has to be promoted with euphemisms, that may be because the use of accurate, descriptive language would demonstrate that the policy is misguided.

NOT JUST FOR THE TERMINALLY ILL

10. Wouldn't euthanasia only be available to people who are terminally ill?

Absolutely not. There are two problems here—the definition of "terminal" and the changes that have already taken place to extend euthanasia to those who aren't "terminally ill."

There are many definitions for the word "terminal." For example, when he spoke to the National Press Club in 1992, Jack Kevorkian said that a terminal illness was "any disease that curtails life even for a day." The co-founder of the Hemlock Society often refers to "terminal old age." Some laws define "terminal" condition as one from which death will occur in a "relatively short time." Others state that "terminal" means that death is expected within six months or less.

Even where a specific life expectancy (like six months) is referred to, medical experts acknowledge that it is virtually impossible to predict the life expectancy of a particular patient. Moreover, some people diagnosed as terminally ill don't die for years, if at all, from the diagnosed condition.

Increasingly, however, euthanasia activists have dropped references to terminal illness, replacing them with such phrases as "hopelessly ill," "desperately ill," "incurably ill," "hopeless condition," and "meaningless life."

An article in the journal *Suicide and Life-Threatening Behavior* described assisted suicide guidelines for those with a hopeless condition. "Hopeless condition" was defined to include terminal illness, severe physical or psychological pain, physical or mental debilitation or deterioration, or a quality of life that is no longer acceptable to the individual. That means just about anybody who has a suicidal impulse .

In a May 1996 speech to the prestigious American Psychiatric

Association, George Delury (who assisted in the 1995 death of his wife who had multiple sclerosis) suggested that "hopelessly ill people or people past age sixty just apply for a license to die" and that such a license should be granted without examination by doctors.

THE SICK AND THE ELDERLY WILL BE PRESSURED INTO EUTHANASIA

11. Wouldn't euthanasia only be at a patient's request?

No. As one of their major arguments, euthanasia proponents claim that euthanasia should be considered "medical treatment." If one accepts the notion that euthanasia is good, then it would not only be inappropriate, but discriminatory, to deny this "good" to a person solely on the basis of that person's being too young or too mentally incapacitated to make the request.

In fact, a surrogate's decision is often treated, for legal purposes, as if it had been made by the patient. That means children and people who can't make their own decisions could well be euthanized.

Suppose, however, that surrogates were not permitted to choose death for another. The problem of how free a death request would be still remains.

If euthanasia becomes accepted in policy or in practice, subtle, even unintended, coercion will be unavoidable.

12. Could euthanasia become a means of health care cost containment?

Perhaps one of the most important developments in recent years is the increasing emphasis placed on health care providers to contain costs. In such a climate, euthanasia certainly could become a means of cost containment.

In the United States, thousands of people have no medical insurance; studies have shown that the poor and minorities generally are not given access to available pain control, and managed-care facilities are offering physicians cash bonuses if they don't provide care for patients.

With greater and greater emphasis being placed on managed care, many doctors are at financial risk when they provide treatment for their patients.

Legalized euthanasia raises the potential for a profoundly dangerous situation in which doctors could find themselves far better off financially if a seriously ill or disabled person "chooses" to die rather than receive long-term care.

Savings to the government may also become a consideration. This could take place if governments cut back on paying for treatment and care and replace them with the "treatment" of death.

For example, immediately after the passage of Measure 16, Oregon's law permitting assisted suicide, Jean Thorne, the state's Medicaid Director, announced that physician-assisted suicide would be paid for as "comfort care" under the Oregon Health Plan which provides medical coverage for about 345,000 poor Oregonians.

Within eighteen months of Measure 16's passage, the State of Oregon announced plans to cut back on health care coverage for poor state residents.

In Canada, hospital stays are being shortened while, at the same time, funds have not been made available for home care for the sick and elderly.

Registered nurses are being replaced with less expensive practical nurses. Patients are forced to endure long waits for many types of needed surgery.

Reprinted by permission of Chuck Asay and Creators Syndicate.

13. Certainly no one would be forced into euthanasia, would they?

Physical force is highly unlikely. But emotional and psychological pressures could become overpowering for depressed or dependent people. If the choice of euthanasia is considered as good as a decision to receive care, many people will feel guilty for not choosing death.

Financial considerations, added to the concern about "being a burden," could serve as powerful forces that would lead a person to "choose" euthanasia or assisted suicide.

Even the smallest gesture could create a gentle nudge into the grave. Such was evidenced in greeting cards sold at the 1991 national conference of the Hemlock Society.

According to the conference program, the cards were designed to be given to those who are terminally ill. One card in particular exemplified the core of the movement that would remove the last shred of hope remaining to a person faced with a life-threatening illness. It carried the message, "I learned you'll be leaving us soon."

PAIN AND DEPRESSION CAN BE TREATED

14. If death is inevitable, shouldn't a person who is dying and wants to commit suicide have the right to do so?

It's really important to understand that suicide in a person who has been diagnosed with a terminal illness is no different than suicide for someone who is not considered terminally ill. Depression, family conflict, feelings of abandonment, hopelessness, etc. lead to suicide—regardless of one's physical condition.

Studies have shown that if pain and depression are adequately treated in a dying person—as they would be in a suicidal nondying person—the desire to commit suicide evaporates.

Suicide among the terminally ill, like suicide among the population in general, is a tragic event that cuts short the life of the victim and leaves devastated survivors.

15. Isn't euthanasia sometimes the only way to relieve excruciating pain?

Quite the contrary. Euthanasia activists exploit the natural fear people have of suffering and dying, and often imply that when cure is no longer likely, there are only two alternatives: euthanasia or unbearable pain.

For example, an official of Choice in Dying, a right-to-die organization, said refusing to permit euthanasia "would, in fact, be to abandon the patient to a horrifying death."

Such an irresponsible statement fails to note that virtually all pain can be eliminated and that—in those rare cases where it can't be eliminated—it can still be reduced significantly if proper treatment is provided.

It is a national and international scandal that so many people do not get adequate pain control. But killing is not the answer to that scandal. The solution is to mandate better education of health care professionals on these crucial issues, to expand access to health care, and to inform patients about their rights as consumers.

Everyone—whether it be a person with a life-threatening illness or a chronic condition—has the right to pain relief. With modern advances in pain control, no patient should ever be in excruciating pain. However, most doctors have never had a course in pain management so they're unaware of what to do.

If a patient who is under a doctor's care is in excruciating pain, there's definitely a need to find a different doctor. But that doctor should be one who will control the pain, not one who will kill the patient.

There are board certified specialists in pain management who will not only help alleviate physical pain but are skilled in providing necessary support to deal with emotional suffering and depression that often accompanies physical pain.

Not Just a Religious Issue

16. Isn't opposition to euthanasia just an attempt to impose religious beliefs on others?

No. Euthanasia leaders have attempted for a long time to make it seem that anyone against euthanasia is trying to impose his or her own religion on society. But that's not the case.

People on both sides of the euthanasia controversy claim membership in religious denominations. There are also individuals on both sides who claim no religious affiliation at all. But it's even more important to realize that this is not a religious debate. It's a debate about public policy and the law.

The fact that the religious convictions of some people parallel what has been long-standing public policy does not disqualify them from taking a stand on an issue.

For example, there are laws that prohibit sales clerks from stealing company profits. Although these laws coincide with religious beliefs, it would be absurd to suggest that such laws should be eliminated. And it would be equally ridiculous to say that a person who has religious opposition to stealing shouldn't be able to support laws against stealing.

Likewise, the fact that the religious convictions of some euthanasia opponents parallel what has been long-standing public policy does not disqualify them from taking a stand on the issue.

Throughout all of modern history, laws have prohibited mercy killing. The need for such laws has been, and should continue to be, debated on the basis of public policy, and people of any or no religious belief should have the right to be involved in that debate.

In Washington State, where an attempt to legalize euthanasia and assisted suicide failed in 1991, polls taken within days of the vote indicated that fewer than ten percent of those who opposed the measure had done so for religious reasons.

The following year, voters in California turned down a similar proposal. During the campaign, euthanasia leaders claimed that all opposition was religious, yet the groups opposing the measure that would have legalized euthanasia and assisted suicide included the California Commission on Aging, California Medical Association, California Nurses Association, California Psychiatric Association and the California State Hospice Association. In addition, all major newspapers throughout the state, including the *Los Angeles Times*, *San Francisco Chronicle*, and *San Diego Union-Tribune* took strong editorial positions against the measure.

KEEP EUTHANASIA ILLEGAL

17. Where does the main support for euthanasia come from?

While the most visible and vocal support for euthanasia and assisted suicide comes from individuals like Jack Kevorkian or "right-to-die" organizations, groups and individuals concerned about lowering health care costs are becoming increasingly involved in euthanasia advocacy. For example, some foundations with links to profit-making health care enterprises fund programs with a distinct pro-euthanasia bias.

18. Since suicide isn't against the law, why should it be illegal to help someone commit suicide?

Neither suicide nor attempted suicide are criminalized anywhere in the United States or in many other countries, but not because of any "right" to suicide. When penalties against attempted suicide were removed, legal scholars made it clear that this was not done for the purpose of permitting suicide. Instead it was intended to prevent suicide. By removing penalties people could seek help in dealing with the problems they're facing without risk of being prosecuted if it were discovered that they had attempted suicide.

Just as current public policy does not grant a "right" to be killed to a person who is suicidal because of a lost business, neither should it permit people to be killed because they are in despair over their physical condition. If euthanasia were legalized, condemned killers would have more rights to have their lives protected than would vulnerable people who could be coerced, pressured and exploited into what amounts to capital punishment for the "crime" of being old, sick, disabled, or dependent.

19. Where is euthanasia legal?

At the present time, the State of Oregon has the world's only law specifically permitting a doctor to prescribe lethal drugs for the purpose of ending a patient's life.

Although euthanasia is widely practiced in the Netherlands, it remains technically illegal.

In 1995 Australia's Northern Territory approved a euthanasia bill. It went into effect in 1996 and was overturned by the Australian Parliament in 1997.

PERIODICAL BIBLIOGRAPHY

The following articles have been selected to supplement the diverse views presented in this chapter. Addresses are provided for periodicals not indexed in the *Readers' Guide to Periodical Literature*, the *Alternative Press Index*, the *Social Sciences Index*, or the *Index to Legal Periodicals and Books*.

Robert H. Bork "Killing for Convenience: Abortion, Assisted Suicide, and Euthanasia," *Human Life Review*, Winter 1997. Available from 215 Lexington Ave., 4th Floor, New York, NY 10016.

Dudley Clendinen "When Death Is a Blessing and Life Is Not," *New York Times*, February 5, 1996.

John Bookser Feister "Thou Shalt Not Kill: The Church Against Assisted Suicide," *St. Anthony Messenger*, June 1997. Available from 1615 Republican St., Cincinnati, OH 45210.

John Hardwig "Is There a Duty to Die?" *Hastings Center Report*, March/April 1997.

Patrick D. Hopkins "Why Does Removing Machines Count as 'Passive' Euthanasia?" *Hastings Center Report*, May/June 1997.

Richard A. McCormick *"Vive La Difference! Killing and Allowing to Die,"* *America*, December 6, 1997.

Arthur Rifkin "Spiritual Aspects of Physician-Assisted Suicide," *Friends Journal*, October 1997. Available from 1216 Arch St., 2A, Philadelphia, PA 19107-2835.

Nancy Shute "Death with More Dignity," *U.S. News & World Report*, February 24, 1997.

Andrew Solomon "A Death of One's Own," *New Yorker*, May 22, 1998.

John Shelby Spong "In Defense of Assisted Suicide," *Human Quest*, May/June 1996. Available from 4300 NW 23rd Ave., Box 203, Gainesville, FL 32614-7050.

USA Today "The American Way of Death," special section, January 1996.

Adam Wolfson "Killing Off the Dying?" *Public Interest*, Spring 1998.

SHOULD VOLUNTARY EUTHANASIA BE LEGALIZED?

CHAPTER PREFACE

In March 1996, the Ninth Circuit Court of Appeals ruled that Washington State's law banning physician-assisted suicide (PAS) was unconstitutional. The court proclaimed that the Constitution protects the right of terminally ill patients to receive medications for the purpose of committing suicide. In April 1996, the Second Circuit Court of Appeals declared that a similar ban in New York State was also unconstitutional. These rulings were heralded as major victories by those within the right-to-die movement.

However, in early 1997 both the Washington and New York cases were appealed before the Supreme Court. In June of that year the Court issued a unanimous decision, upholding the bans on assisted suicide in both states. In rejecting the lower courts' decisions, the justices of the Supreme Court effectively ruled that there is no constitutionally protected right to die.

Opponents of euthanasia commend the Court's caution: Columnist John Leo characterizes the decision as "a very dangerous step not taken." "For once, at least," writes Leo, "an urgent moral and political debate was not swept aside by a court determined to give us the correct answer from on high." Legal experts agree that the controversy over PAS will continue, but law professor Yale Kamisar contends that "There are only so many arguments in favor of a 'right' to PAS, and almost all were addressed by the Court. . . . These arguments have lost a considerable amount of credibility and will be easier to rebuff when made again."

Although the Court's decision was a clear setback for the right-to-die movement, advocates have not lost heart. Columnist Ellen Goodman declares that "Sooner or later, one way or another, the practice will become legal." Proponents note that although the Court did not recognize a constitutional right to PAS, they did not create a federal ban on the practice either. Instead, the matter has been left to the states to decide. Euthanasia activists have vowed to continue the battle over PAS in state legislatures: "If we have to win this right state by state, then so be it," says Compassion in Dying president Susan Dunshee.

As legislators across the country choose whether to legalize or ban physician-assisted suicide in their states, they must consider public opinion, the plight of the terminally ill, and the potential risks that PAS entails. The authors in the following chapter debate these and other legal issues surrounding voluntary euthanasia.

"Providing physician-assisted dying
for a terminally ill, mentally
competent adult who requests it is a
humane, compassionate, safe and
effective option which should be
made legal."

VOLUNTARY EUTHANASIA SHOULD BE LEGALIZED

Faye J. Girsh

In the following viewpoint, Faye Girsh argues that it should be
legal for doctors to respect the wishes of terminally ill individuals who request assistance in committing suicide. A majority of
Americans support the legalization of assisted suicide, Girsh
claims. She maintains that physicians already help patients to
die; legalizing the practice, in her view, would make it subject to
safety regulations and less prone to abuse. Girsh insists that
physician-assisted suicide is consistent with a doctor's obligation to relieve suffering, and that the option would be limited to
the terminally ill. Faye Girsh is director of the Hemlock Society,
a national right-to-die organization based in Denver, Colorado.

As you read, consider the following questions:

1. According to the poll that Girsh cites, what percent of people
   over fifty-five agreed that terminally ill people have a right to
   commit suicide with a doctor's assistance?
2. In Girsh's view, what is the major shortcoming of advance
   directives?
3. According to the author, how is a mockery being made of
   existing law?

Reprinted from Faye J. Girsh, "The Case for Physician Aid in Dying," *Journal of the
Hippocratic Society*, Fall 1997, by permission of the author. (References in the original have
been omitted in this reprint.)

On June 26, 1997, the U.S. Supreme Court issued a unanimously ambivalent opinion saying that there is no right to physician-assisted dying under the 14th Amendment, but that it is a matter to be left to state legislatures.

Rather than putting a stop to the debate, the decision has raised the volume of dialogue, which will increase as citizens vote on ballot initiatives and legislators introduce bills permitting physician aid in dying. Especially for the past five years, the American public has been deluged with journal and newspaper articles, TV coverage, books, court decisions, jury verdicts, surveys, referenda, legislation—more than the average person can follow. One fortunate fallout of the controversy has been greater attention to the care of the terminally ill.

The right-to-die issue rivals the abortion controversy in capturing public attention; after enabling legislation is passed, the divisiveness about the issue will not disappear since there is a strong, religiously dominated minority who see both issues as a threat to the sanctity of life and who will continue to rail against choice in these areas.

THE HEMLOCK SOCIETY

As with most other strongly held beliefs, there are advocacy organizations for both sides. The Hemlock Society was founded in 1980, shortly after the first "living will law" was passed in California in 1976; since then other organizations have developed. The mission of the Hemlock Society is to maximize the options for a dignified death, including voluntary physician aid in dying for terminally ill, mentally competent adults.

When the Hemlock Society was founded, "passive euthanasia" was just becoming acceptable, i.e., letting a patient die by refusal or removal of life support. It was a decade later that the Supreme Court, albeit weakly, affirmed the right of all Americans to refuse or withdraw unwanted medical treatment, including food and hydration, and to have an agent speak for them if they were incompetent. But that is not enough, since many patients who stop treatment die a prolonged and agonizing death and others do not have treatment to remove and so have no way to hasten their deaths.

ATTEMPTS TO LEGALIZE PHYSICIAN AID IN DYING

Although there had been perfunctory legislation unsuccessfully introduced in the first half of this century, it was in 1988 that the recent attempts to pass laws permitting physician aid in dying began. In California the Humane and Dignified Death Act was proposed but did not get enough signatures to get on the ballot. In 1991, 46% of the voters in Washington supported Proposition 119. The following year a similar ballot measure, Proposition 161, was placed before the people of California and also received 46% of the vote. Both campaigns were expensive and heated; advocates of physician aid in dying were outspent three to one, with the money for opposing physician aid in dying coming primarily from Catholic sources. In 1994, 51% of the people of Oregon voted to permit physician aid in dying, using a prescribing-only model, but the Oregon Death with Dignity law has been tied up in the Courts since then and has not gone into effect. The Oregon legislature voted to turn it back to the people in a repeal vote which will be taken on November 4, 1997. [Voters rejected the measure to repeal the law, and physician-assisted suicide is currently legal in Oregon.]

The issue is not one which affects just Americans. Since 1984 the Dutch have permitted physician-assisted suicide under strict judicial guidelines although no law has been passed. In Switzerland about 120 people on average have died each year with the help of physicians and members of the Exit Society following a law passed there 60 years ago allowing euthanasia if the intent is benign. The Northern Territory of Australia, under the Rights of the Terminally Ill Act, permitted four people with cancer to die with the help of a doctor from July 1996 to December 1996 before the law was repealed by the federal parliament. In Colombia, a Catholic country, the Constitutional Court ruled that mercy killing should be decriminalized.

Why the growing consensus? Below I will list the reasons the Hemlock Society—and the majority of Americans polled—believe that providing physician-assisted dying for a terminally ill, mentally competent adult who requests it is a humane, compassionate, safe and effective option which should be made legal.

Eighteen Reasons for Legalization

1. It is inhumane, cruel and even barbaric to make a suffering person, whose death is inevitable, live longer than he or she wishes. It is the final decision a person makes; there must be autonomy at that time of life if at no other. To quote legal philosopher Ronald Dworkin: "Making someone die in a way that others approve, but he believes is a horrifying contradiction of his life, is a devastating, odious form of tyranny."

2. It is necessary for physicians to be the agents of death if the person wants to die quickly, safely, peacefully and nonviolently since the best means to accomplish this is medication that

only doctors can prescribe. There is no prohibition against a person killing oneself. In a civilized society a person should be able to die quickly with dignity and certainty in the company of loved ones, if that is her wish. Methods at the individual's disposal, however, are usually violent and uncertain, as well as traumatizing to the patient and the family.

Ironically, the moral and ethical objections to hastening death do not concern self-deliverance. There is little concern in the dialogues about the fact that people choose to hasten their deaths. It is about the role of the doctor and the ethics and legality of providing assistance. There is little dialogue about a person who is not a doctor providing help, although this too is illegal since it is still assisted suicide.

PUBLIC OPINION ON ASSISTED SUICIDE

Respondents were asked to pick which of the following statements came closest to their views on legalizing physician-assisted suicide.

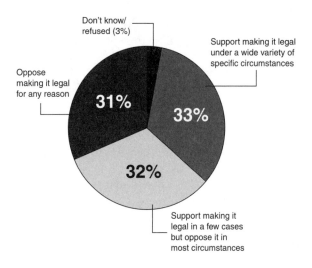

Don't know/ refused (3%)

Support making it legal under a wide variety of specific circumstances

Oppose making it legal for any reason

31%

33%

32%

Support making it legal in a few cases but oppose it in most circumstances

George H. Gallup International Institute, *Spiritual Beliefs and the Dying Process*, 1998.

3. A dying person who wishes to hasten her inevitable death does not cause the same repercussions as someone who is committing suicide, as we know it. Suicide, as we think of it, occurs in a person who is emotionally unstable and has a problem that will go away with time and/or intervention. It has been called a permanent solution to a temporary problem. Suicide traumatizes survivors because of the guilt they feel that they could have

helped, that they were not able to talk about it, that the death was sudden and often violent and that there would have been a long, fulfilling life ahead if the person had changed his or her mind. With a terminally ill person, if physician-assisted dying were legal, the family could be present, good-byes could be said, and the death could be, as some family members who have openly participated describe it, a "wonderful" experience. And there would be no guilt that the person could have lived a full life had the hastened death not occurred since it would be at the patient's request, usually with the consultation of the family, and in the context of terminal illness.

PUBLIC OPINION SUPPORTS LEGALIZATION

4. A significant majority of Americans favor legalizing physician aid in dying for terminally ill people who request it and this number has increased steadily.

In a democratic society it is the case that laws follow the will of the people. In this case lawmakers have been intimidated by the force of the religious objections and have ducked the issue thus far.

5. Disabled, poor, elderly and minority people also want to die a good death. Polls of disabled individuals show a majority in support. A 1994 Harris poll found 66% of people with disabilities surveyed support a right to assisted dying. Between 63% and 90% of people with AIDS want this option and 55% have considered it for themselves. Two articles by influential disabled individuals [Andrew Batavia in the *New England Journal of Medicine* and Barry Corbet in *New Mobility*] indicate their reasoning in favoring legal physician aid in dying.

Support is also strong from older Americans. A 1996 survey by *RxRemedy Magazine* of more than 30,000 people over 55 showed that 65% agreed that terminally people had a right to commit suicide with a doctor's assistance.

In the guise of protecting these groups, opponents argue that they would be hurt by an assisted dying law since they would be vulnerable. This "protection" not only deprives people who are not in these categories of choice and dignity in dying, it robs those very groups of this option with no evidence that this is a choice they would not want. In fact, evidence suggests that all people want this option, regardless of their status.

PHYSICIANS HAVE A DUTY TO RELIEVE SUFFERING

6. It is consistent with a doctor's role to relieve suffering and to do no harm. Few doctors now take the actual Hippocratic Oath,

which is irrelevant in many respects to modem medicine. Relief of suffering is the major objective of medicine; in the final extremes of a patient's life, the only way to relieve suffering may be to comply with a patient's wish for death. Many patients would trust a doctor more who would offer them all alternatives at life's end than those who would stop short of granting them their wish. What is likely is that patients and doctors do not have a dialogue about this and that physician aid in dying would actually enhance the doctor-patient relationship.

7. Physicians are helping patients die now with no monitoring or controls. They cannot contact consultants or openly discuss their choices. A recent study of physicians in San Francisco who work with AIDS patients showed that 53% provided help in dying.

Surveys of doctors also show support for legalization. Fifty-four percent of Washington State physicians surveyed agreed physician aid in dying should be legal under some conditions. In Oregon 60% of physicians agreed and 66% agreed in Michigan.

8. Religious opinions about the sanctity of life would be respected. People who do not want a hastened death would not have to have one. However, there are many ways of hastening death, or at least not extending life, which are approved by religious groups including refusal of treatment including food and hydration, hospice, and the double effect (providing enough pain medication to end suffering without the direct intention of causing death, even if death is a result). Even groups most passionately concerned about the sanctity of life, which at one time raised concerns about refusal of treatment, have come to a position that quantity of life considerations must be balanced against quality of life realities. Surveys which have analyzed their results by religious preference show that at least 50% of Catholics favor this; one survey finds up to 72% of Catholics endorse the idea.

ASSISTED DYING IS COMPATIBLE WITH HOSPICE CARE

9. Palliative care would not be precluded. Most of us do not want to make the choice between compassionate hospice care, which could provide excellent pain relief, and the option of asking for a hastened death if pain and suffering were unbearable. Nobody seems to argue that all dying patients should have the option to refuse heroic measures, should receive the best pain relief available, and should have access to hospice services. The debate is whether there also must be a choice between hospice and assisted dying. Janet Good, former president of the Hemlock Society of Michigan, died recently of pancreatic cancer while under the excellent care of the Angela Hospice and apparently

with the help of Dr. Kevorkian. It seems logical, in fact, for some non-religious hospices to provide the help desired by a small percentage of their patients.

THE ULTIMATE CIVIL RIGHT

We in the right-to-die movement are determined to put an end to the anguish being unjustly inflicted upon the dying and their loved ones. The obscenity of the state denying its citizens the ultimate human and civil right to own and control their own lives and bodies is intolerable. Surely our intrinsic right of self-determination must include the next breath we draw. We are not arguing for a limitlessly broad right to die.

We seek to secure the right of mentally competent, terminally ill individuals to choose a death with dignity and without needless suffering.

Barbara Dority, Humanist, July/August 1997.

---

10. There would be no progression beyond what public policy dictated. Terminally ill, mentally competent adults is the category of individuals we are generally talking about now, although some proposals have included people with hopeless illnesses. We have not had a chance to see how this model of physician aid in dying will work; it is premature to consider expanding the law at this point. Slippery slopes are neither predictable nor preventable; it is pointless to argue that allowing this limited model of help for dying, competent adults will inevitably lead to other consequences which are undesirable for the society.

REFUSAL OF TREATMENT IS NOT ENOUGH

11. Refusal of treatment is not enough and is morally equivalent to asking for help in dying. Many people feel that they are protected because they have an advance directive. This only permits refusal or termination of treatment. It will not assure that death will not be prolonged and agonizing. In the situation of refusal or treatment the wish of the patient is to end life. It is often the fortunate patient who can "pull the plug"; for those who do not have a plug, assisted dying is the humane and ethically equivalent solution.

12. People would live longer and better knowing there is help if the suffering becomes unbearable. The anxiety of not knowing how much longer one would have to suffer and watch the family suffer adds to the burden of terminal illness. Many

people must end their lives prematurely through suicide while they are still able. Life could be extended if they knew help would be available from a physician.

13. Not all pain can be controlled. Even taking the best estimate from hospice, that 97% of pain is controllable, that still leaves 3% of dying people whose pain is unrelievable. What help is there for them? And, not all suffering is caused by physical pain. Surveys of patients in Holland who request aid in dying show that pain is fifth on the list of reasons why they ask for a hastened death. It is "senseless suffering" and the indignities of dependency, incontinence, and poor quality of life which lead them to request a hastened death. In addition, not all patients want the consequences of adequate pain control, which include diminution of cognitive function and severe constipation.

AID IN DYING MUST BE REGULATED

14. Physician aid in dying is commonly practiced today in the United States. Doctors have always helped their patients end their suffering. If we are concerned about abuse of this practice, there should be controls and monitoring. In addition, it is a disservice to those people who cannot get help because they lack a personal relationship to their doctor, or who have a doctor who is unwilling to risk legal action and loss of license. No doctor has ever been convicted for helping a patient die, but those who do help often have to experience horrendous legal hassles before they are acquitted. Aid in dying must be regulated, legalized and aboveboard so that doctors, families and patients can discuss it as part of the continuum of care. The process and criteria should be regulated and the outcomes reported. This is the way to prevent abuses and stop the slippery slope—not by driving it underground.

15. The issue will not go away. Increasingly, people are dying of chronic, debilitating illnesses such as cancer, neurological diseases, AIDS, and heart disease. This means longer periods of suffering and a prolongation of the dying process. People fear this extended dependency and want to know there is an end about which they can make a determination.

16. Physician aid in dying is not a significant cost-cutting measure. What we know from Holland is that life is reduced by a matter of days when physician intervention occurs. It is more of a cost-saving when treatment is refused, so there would be an incentive for managed care organizations to encourage patients to refuse or terminate life-saving treatments or even to refer them prematurely for hospice care. There is no hue and cry

about this and certainly no suggestion that we should rescind the right to refuse treatment or hospice because of the possible coercion that people might be experiencing from the physician or the insurance carrier.

THE CURRENT SITUATION IS WORSE

17. The abuses of not permitting lawful aid in dying far outweigh any that would arise if a carefully safeguarded law were in place. What we have now are botched attempts, trauma to the family, needless suffering on the part of patients and their loved ones, doctors who are helping without any type of oversight, and juries who acquit physicians and loved ones who help. Above all, there is an injustice to a dying individual who is denied the ultimate choice of deciding the time and manner of her death.

18. A mockery is made of the existing law. No doctor has been convicted in this country for helping a patient die. Juries routinely acquit physicians and loved ones who provide compassionate help and most cases are not even charged or brought to trial. The principle of double effect is used as a "don't ask, don't tell" situation where medication is given to hasten death but the "intention" is only to relieve suffering. This means doctors and patients cannot discuss it; patients who would like help are wary of putting their doctors in a criminal situation.

There is no question that physician aid in dying will eventually be an option for people who live in developed countries where chronic diseases are the major cause of death. People want this, doctors want it; it can be regulated, and individuals in a free world must be able to decide this ultimate question about their lives.

> "Few slogans are more stirring than the right to die. But few phrases are more fuzzy, more misleading, or more misunderstood."

VOLUNTARY EUTHANASIA SHOULD NOT BE LEGALIZED

Yale Kamisar

In the following viewpoint, Yale Kamisar discusses why he believes people support assisted suicide, and he explains why he finds popular pro-euthanasia arguments unconvincing. Kamisar contends that voluntary euthanasia cannot be safely regulated and that, if legalized, it cannot reasonably be limited to the terminally ill. Moreover, he maintains that even if euthanasia might help some terminally ill patients, it should still remain illegal because legalizing it would pressure others to choose suicide. Yale Kamisar is a professor at the University of Michigan Law School in Ann Arbor.

As you read, consider the following questions:

1. Why does Kamisar believe that examining the plight of a suffering, terminally ill individual is not the best way to understand the issue of legalizing assisted suicide and euthanasia?
2. Why do Daniel Callahan and Margot White, as paraphrased by the author, believe that laws regulating assisted suicide would be ineffective?
3. What are the four different "rights to die," according to Kamisar?

Excerpted from Yale Kamisar, "The Reasons So Many People Support Physician-Assisted Suicide—and Why These Reasons Are Not Convincing," *Issues in Law & Medicine*, vol. 12, no. 2, Fall 1996. Reprinted with permission of the publisher. Copyright ©1996 by the National Legal Center for the Medically Dependent & Disabled, Inc. (Footnotes in the original have been omitted in this reprint.)

It would be hard to deny that there is a great deal of support in this country—and ever-growing support—for legalizing physician-assisted suicide (PAS). Why is this so? I believe there are a considerable number of reasons. In this article, I shall discuss [four] common reasons and explain why I do not find any of them convincing.

THE COMPELLING FORCE OF HEARTRENDING INDIVIDUAL CASES

Many people, understandably, are greatly affected by the heart-wrenching facts of individual cases, e.g., a person enduring the last stages of ALS (Lou Gehrig's disease), who gasps: "I want . . . I want . . . to die." In this regard the media, quite possibly inadvertently, advances the cause of PAS.

A reporter often thinks that the way to provide in-depth coverage of the subject of assisted suicide and euthanasia is to provide a detailed account of a particular person suffering from a particular disease and asking: "How can we deny this person the active intervention of another to bring about death?" Or "What would you want done if you were in this person's shoes?" But we should not let a compelling individual case blot out more general considerations. The issue is not simply what seems best for the individual who is the focal point of a news story, but what seems best for society as a whole.

LEGALIZATION WOULD AFFECT EVERYONE

Everyone interested in the subject of PAS and active voluntary euthanasia (AVE) has heard emotional stories about people suffering great pain and begging for someone to kill them or help them bring about their death. But people like Kathleen Foley, the Memorial Sloan-Kettering Cancer Center's renowned pain control expert, and Herbert Hendin, the American Suicide Foundation's executive director, can tell very moving stories, too—stories militating against the legalization of PAS and AVE. They can tell us how suicidal ideation and suicide requests commonly dissolve with adequate control of pain and other symptoms or how, for example, after much conversation with a caring physician, a suicidal patient—one who had become convinced that suicide or assisted suicide was his best option—changed his mind, how his desperation subsided, and how he used the remaining months of his life to become closer to his wife and parents.

I can hear the cries of protest now. "Let terminally ill people (and perhaps others as well) obtain assistance in committing suicide if that is what they want. They're not bothering anybody else. Letting them determine the time and manner of their death won't affect anybody else."

But I am afraid it will. . . .

This article is being written at a time when the firmly established right to refuse or to terminate lifesaving medical treatment is being used as a launching pad for a right to PAS. However the issue of assisted suicide is ultimately resolved, it will reflect society's views about life and death, as did resolution of the debate over disconnecting the respirator and pulling the feeding tube.

THE ILLUSION OF PATIENT AUTONOMY

Many want to believe—and loose talk about the "right to die" encourages them to do so—that the termination of life support for dying or seriously ill patients, a considerable number of whom are no longer competent, is merely an exercise of individual autonomy. But, as professor Donald Beschle writes, "medical technology has forced the law to resolve questions concerning termination of medical treatment . . . by making largely social decisions involving our attitudes toward life, and the ways in which society allocates resources best to preserve it and its quality." That many of us prefer to believe that we have simply been deferring to personal autonomy is hardly surprising. On the one hand, confronting questions about the quality of life "worth" preserving is discomfiting, even frightening; on the other hand, individual autonomy is highly prized in our society. But, says Beschle, "this model of mere deference to individual wishes does not ring true in many 'right to die' cases."

Although I sometimes disagree strongly with Professor Charles Baron, a leading proponent of physician-assisted suicide, I share his view that in many, probably most, persistent vegetative state cases "what actually drives death decisions . . . is an objective test based an the convergence of 'best interests' and economic criteria. [But] the extreme discomfort of making death decisions for other people and our fear of the slippery slope . . . lead us to pretend that we are merely complying (however reluctantly) with the wishes of the patient. The result in most states is mere lip service to substituted judgment."

FROM A RIGHT TO DIE TO A DUTY TO DIE

More generally, as Professor Donald Beschle has pointed out:

> One way or the other, . . . society will label certain types of decisions about death as 'right' and others as 'wrong,' some as courageous and noble, others as at least disappointing, possibly cow-

ardly, or even disgraceful. These social labels cannot fail to influence subsequent individual choices. In addition, such attitudes can cause decision makers to interpret the statements and actions of the individual patient in ways that are at least problematic.

The "right to die" is a catchy rallying cry, but here as elsewhere we should, in the words of author Paul A. Freund, "turn up [our] collars against windy sloganeering, no matter from which direction it is blown." The right to die focuses on what is only one aspect of a multi-dimensional problem. I think law professor Seth Kreimer put it well when he summarized the "fearsome dilemma" presented by the assisted suicide issue as follows:

> Forbidding [assisted suicide] leaves some citizens with the prospect of being trapped in agony or indignity from which they could be delivered by a death they desire. But permitting such assistance risks the unwilling or manipulated death of the most vulnerable members of society, and the erosion of the normative structure that encourages them, their families, and their doctors to choose life.

EUTHANASIA CANNOT BE EFFECTIVELY REGULATED

. . . Another argument for PAS that appeals to a goodly number of people goes something like this: A significant number of physicians have been performing assisted suicide anyway, so why not legalize it? Wouldn't it be better to bring the practice out in the open and to formulate clear standards than to keep the practice underground and unregulated?

It is not at all clear how prevalent the underground practice is. As Daniel Callahan, president of the Hastings Center, and Margot White, a lawyer specializing in bioethics, have pointed out, however, if it is truly the case that current laws against euthanasia (and assisted suicide) are widely ignored by doctors, "why should we expect new statutes to be taken with greater moral and legal seriousness?" Evidently no physician has ever been convicted of a crime for helping a suffering patient die at her request. But, as Callahan and White ask, why should we expect that there will be any more convictions for violating the new laws than there have been for violating the laws presently in effect?

What Dr. Herbert Hendin warned a 1996 congressional subcommittee in his testimony about the impact of legalizing euthanasia applies to the legalization of PAS as well: Absent "an intrusion into the relationship between patient and doctor that most patients would not want and most doctors would not accept," no law or set of guidelines covering euthanasia (or assisted suicide) *can* protect patients. Adds Dr. Hendin:

> After euthanasia [or assisted suicide] has been performed, since only the patient and the doctor may know the actual facts of the case, and since only the doctor is alive to relate them, any medical, legal, or interdisciplinary review committee will, as in the Netherlands, only know what the doctor chooses to tell them. Legal sanction creates a permissive atmosphere that seems to foster not taking the guidelines too seriously. The notion that those American doctors—who are admittedly breaking some serious laws in now assisting in a suicide—would follow guidelines if assisted suicide were legalized is not borne out by the Dutch experience; nor is it likely given the failure of American practitioners of assisted suicide to follow elementary safeguards in cases they have published.

FAULTY REASONING IN THE COURTS

In March 1996, in the course of ruling that mentally competent, terminally ill patients, at least, have a constitutionally protected right to assisted suicide, an 8-3 majority of the U.S. Court of Appeals for the Ninth Circuit (covering California, Washington, Oregon, and other western states) wrote that it could see "no ethical or constitutionally cognizable difference between a doctor's pulling the plug on a respirator and his prescribing drugs which will permit a terminally ill patient to end his own life." According to the Ninth Circuit, the important thing is that "the death of the patient is the intended result as surely in one case as in the other." Thus, the Ninth Circuit found "the state's interests in preventing suicide do not make its interests substantially stronger here than in cases involving other forms of death-hastening medical intervention."

The Ninth Circuit found the right to assisted suicide grounded in the due process clause. A month later, a three-judge panel of the U.S. Court of Appeals for the Second Circuit (covering New York, Connecticut, and Vermont) struck down New York's law against assisted suicide on equal protection grounds.

Although it ultimately arrived at the same result the Ninth Circuit had via a different route, the Second Circuit did so only after "repudiat[ing] the reasoning of Judge Reinhardt's opinion [for the Ninth Circuit], which [it] found open-ended and unconvincing." Nevertheless, the Second Circuit was no more impressed with the alleged distinction between "letting die" and actively intervening to promote or to bring about death than the Ninth Circuit had been.

It "seem[ed] clear" to the Second Circuit that "New York does not treat similarly circumstanced persons alike: those in the final stages of terminal illness who are on life-support systems are allowed to hasten their deaths by directing the removal of such systems; but those who are similarly situated, except for being attached to life-sustaining equipment, are not allowed to [do so] by self-administering prescribed drugs."

THE DANGERS OF LEGALIZATION

Whatever the benefits of legalized physician-assisted suicide and euthanasia, they must be measured against the dangers of legalization. . . . For instance, how would legalization affect our society's already tenuous commitment to providing quality health care for the millions of people who die every year? . . .

Broad legalization of physician-assisted suicide and euthanasia would have the paradoxical effect of making patients seem to be responsible for their own suffering. Rather than being seen primarily as the victims of pain and suffering caused by disease, patients would be seen as having the power to end their suffering by agreeing to an injection or taking some pills; refusing would mean that living through the pain was the patient's decision, the patient's responsibility. Placing the blame on the patient would reduce the motivation of caregivers to provide the extra care that might be required, and would ease guilt if the care fell short. Such an easy, thoughtless shift of responsibility is probably what makes most hospice workers so deeply opposed to physician-assisted suicide and euthanasia.

Ezekiel Emanuel, *Atlantic Monthly*, March 1997.

The Ninth Circuit's due process analysis would seem to apply to active voluntary euthanasia as well as PAS. So would the Second Circuit's equal protection analysis. If persons off life support systems are similarly situated to those on such systems, why aren't terminally ill people who are *unable* to perform the last, death-causing act themselves, and thus need a physician to administer a lethal injection, similarly situated to terminally ill people who *are* able to perform the last, death-causing act themselves?

If a mentally competent, terminally ill person is determined to end her life with the active assistance of another, but needs someone else to administer the lethal medicine, how can she be denied this right simply because she cannot perform the last, death-causing act herself? Applying the reasoning of the Second Circuit, wouldn't denial of the latter person's right or liberty constitute—and at this point I am quoting the very language the

Second Circuit used—a failure to "treat equally all competent persons who are in the final stages of fatal illness and wish to hasten their deaths"?

DIFFERENT KINDS OF RIGHTS TO DIE

I think both the Ninth and Second Circuits went awry by lumping together *different kinds* of rights to die. Few slogans are more stirring than the right to die. But few phrases are more fuzzy, more misleading, or more misunderstood.

The phrase has been used at various times to refer to (a) the right to refuse or to terminate unwanted medical treatment, including lifesaving treatment; (b) the right to commit suicide, at least "rational suicide"; (c) the right to assisted suicide, i.e., the right to obtain another's help in committing suicide; and (d) the right to active voluntary euthanasia, i.e., the right to authorize another to kill you intentionally and directly.

Until March of this year the only kind of right to die any American appellate court, state or federal, had ever established—and the only right or liberty that the New Jersey Supreme Court had recognized in the *Karen Ann Quinlan* case and the Supreme Court had assumed existed in the *Nancy Beth Cruzan* case—was the right to reject life-sustaining medical treatment or, as many have called it, the right to die a natural death. Indeed, the landmark *Quinlan* case had explicitly distinguished between "letting die" on the one hand and both direct killing and assisted suicide an the other.

When all is said and done, both the Second and Ninth Circuit rulings turn largely on the courts' failure to keep two kinds of rights to die separate and distinct—the right to terminate life support and the right to assisted suicide. And their failure to do so indicates that, when faced with the specific issue, they are unlikely to keep a third kind of right to die separate and distinct—active voluntary euthanasia. . . .

WITHDRAWAL OF TREATMENT IS
NOT THE SAME AS ASSISTED DEATH

I believe there are a number of significant differences between the withholding or withdrawal of life-sustaining medical treatment and the active intervention of another to promote or to bring about death. For one thing, as Seth Kreimer has noted, PAS or AVE poses greater dangers to the lives and welfare of persons other than the one before the court than does the rejection of medical treatment:

> [A] right to refuse treatment puts at risk only the lives of those who would die without treatment. While this is a considerable

number of people, the approval of active euthanasia or assisted suicide would extend the risk to the entire population. Particularly with the emergence of cost controls and managed care in the United States, the danger of tempting health care providers to persuade chronic patients to minimize costs by ending it all painlessly is no fantasy. The quantitative distinction between some and all can be a legitimate predicate for the qualitative distinction between permission and prohibition.

PERSONAL AUTONOMY IS NOT ABSOLUTE

Unless we are prepared to carry the principle of "self-determination" or "personal autonomy" or "control of one's destiny" to its ultimate logic—unless we are prepared to say that every competent adult with a firm desire to end her life the way she sees fit for any reason she considers appropriate should have the right or liberty to do so—we have to draw a line somewhere along the way. So why not adhere to the line we had (or the line many of us thought we had) until the Second Circuit and Ninth Circuit handed down their rulings earlier this year?

As I have observed elsewhere, I believe the line between "letting die" and actively intervening to bring about death represents a cultural and pragmatic compromise between the desire to let seriously ill people carry out their wishes to end it all and the felt need to protect the weak and the vulnerable. On the one hand, we want to respect patients' wishes, relieve suffering, and put an end to seemingly futile medical treatment. Hence we allow patients to refuse life-sustaining treatment. On the other hand, we want to affirm the supreme value of life and to maintain the salutary principle that the law protects all human life, no matter how poor its quality. Hence the ban against assisted suicide and active voluntary euthanasia.

It cannot be denied that the two sets of values are in conflict, or at least in great tension. Nevertheless, until very recently at any rate, we have tried to honor both sets of values by permitting a patient to terminate life support but prohibiting active intervention to bring about a patient's death. We should continue to try to do so.

ASSISTED SUICIDE CANNOT BE LIMITED TO THE "TERMINALLY ILL"

Most proponents of the right to PAS speak only of—and for now at least want us to think only about—such a right for terminally ill persons. (Terminal illness is commonly defined as a condition that will produce death "imminently" or "within a short time" or in six months.) Such advocacy is quite understandable.

A proposal to legalize PAS, but to limit that right to terminally ill persons, causes less alarm and commands more general support than would a proposal to establish a broader right to assisted suicide. A proposal to permit only terminally ill patients to enlist the aid of physicians to commit suicide is attractive because it leads the public to believe that adoption of such a proposal would constitute only *a slight* deviation from traditional standards and procedures. And, as Justice Frankfurter once observed, "the function of an advocate is to seduce."

But there are all sorts of reasons why life may seem intolerable to a *reasonable* person. To argue that suicide is plausible or understandable in order to escape intense physical pain or to end a physically debilitated life *but for no other reason* is to show oneself out of touch with the depth arid complexity of human motives.

A few proponents of assisted suicide have taken the position that it would be arbitrary to exclude from coverage persons with incurable, but not terminally ill, progressive illnesses, such as ALS or multiple sclerosis. But why stop there? Is it any less arbitrary to exclude the quadriplegic? The victim of a paralytic stroke? One afflicted with severe arthritis? The disfigured survivor of a fire? The mangled survivor of a road accident? One whose family has been wiped out in an airplane crash?

If personal autonomy and the termination of suffering are supposed to be the touchstones for physician-assisted suicide, why exclude those with nonterminal illnesses or disabilities who might have to endure greater pain and suffering *for much longer periods of time* than those who are expected to die in the next few weeks or months? If terminally ill persons do have a right to assisted suicide, doesn't someone who must continue to live what *she considers* an intolerable or unacceptable existence for many years have an equal, or even greater, right to assisted suicide?

If a *competent* person comes to the unhappy but firm conclusion that her existence is unbearable and freely, clearly, and repeatedly requests assisted suicide, and there is a constitutional right to some form of assisted suicide, why should she be denied the assistance of another to end her life just because she does not qualify under somebody else's standards? Isn't this an arbitrary limitation of self-determination and personal autonomy? . . .

THE WRONG HEALTH CARE RIGHT

Four decades ago, Glanville Williams admitted that he "prepared for ridicule" whenever he described assisted suicide or voluntary euthanasia as "medical operations." "Regarded as surgery," he acknowledged, these practices are "unique, since [their] object is not to save or prolong life but the reverse." Today, few people chuckle when PAS is classified as a medical procedure, or even when it is called a health care right, or even when we are told, at a time when tens of millions of Americans lack adequate health care and Congress has refused to do anything about it, that PAS is the one health care right that deserves constitutional status.

> "Holland has grappled longer and more publicly with the end-of-life issues that we are only now beginning to confront seriously."

LEGALIZED EUTHANASIA IN THE NETHERLANDS HAS NOT HARMED DUTCH SOCIETY

Ellen Goodman

In the following viewpoint, columnist Ellen Goodman describes how physician-assisted suicide is handled in the Netherlands. (It remains technically illegal, but doctors are not prosecuted if they follow certain guidelines.) The author acknowledges several drawbacks to the Dutch policies, and states that they are not appropriate for America. While Goodman maintains that the Dutch approach is not a perfect solution to the complex, divisive problem of euthanasia, she believes the Dutch willingness to acknowledge and deal with the issue is commendable.

As you read, consider the following questions:

1. How do the Dutch define euthanasia, according to Goodman?
2. Why does the author believe that the nine hundred to one thousand annual victims of "non-voluntary euthanasia" are not a result of Holland's euthanasia policies?
3. In the author's opinion, why should America not adopt euthanasia policies similar to those of the Dutch?

Reprinted from Ellen Goodman, "Dutch Deal with Death Their Own Way," *Boston Globe*, April 17, 1997, by permission of the Washington Post Company. ©1997, The Boston Globe Newspaper Co./Washington Post Writers Group.

Halfway through our conversation, Gerrit van der Wal gets up to consult his dictionary. Surely, he says, there must be an English equivalent for the Dutch word "gedogen."

The medical school professor, who conducted the most recent research on doctor-assisted death in the Netherlands, flips through the pages until he comes to the right place. "Gedogen," he reads slowly, "tolerance." Then he shakes his head and says, "No, that isn't quite right."

DUTCH PRAGMATISM

If the word is not easily translated, perhaps it is because the concept is so Dutch, so not-American. Gedogen describes a formal condition somewhere between forbidden and permitted. It is part of the Dutch dance of principle and pragmatism.

Here, drugs are gedogen. They remain illegal, but soft drugs like marijuana and hash are available in duly licensed coffee shops that dot this city.

And here too, euthanasia is gedogen. The ending of a life by a doctor remains illegal, but doctors who follow careful guidelines may grant their patients' death wishes.

I am here in this northern country awash with tulips and controversy because our own Supreme Court has been asked to decide the question of doctor-assisted suicide. Holland has grappled longer and more publicly with the end-of-life issues that we are only now beginning to confront seriously.

As Ad Kerkhof, a puckish psychologist at the Free University, says, "Holland has become a Rorschach test for euthanasia." Indeed, opponents look to Holland and describe this flat country as a land of slippery slopes.

In a week of interviewing, people bristled at the notion that Americans think the Dutch are ridding themselves of the old and handicapped. In fact "euthanasia" is defined here as the termination of life by a doctor at the express wish of a patient. Under the guidelines, the patient's suffering must be unbearable and without the possibility of improvement. The requests must be persistent and confirmed by a second physician.

Van der Wal, warily leading me through his most recent survey of doctors, points out that only 2.4 percent of deaths in Holland happen with a physician's assistance. Nine out of 10 requests are turned away. Most of those who had assisted suicide were not nursing home patients but cancer patients in their 60s or 70s. They died in the last days or weeks of their illness, at home, treated by a family doctor they knew for an average of seven years.

DUTCH TAKE PRIDE IN THEIR SYSTEM DESPITE PROBLEMS

The Dutch system is not fail-safe or without its own ethical dilemmas. Most euthanasia deaths are still (and illegally) not reported to the government. The most troubling discovery is that between 900 and 1,000 patients a year die from what they call "non-voluntary euthanasia."

As doctors here note, a bit defensively, this is not the result of Holland's euthanasia policies. It exists unseen and unreported in countries, even our own, where doctors deliver lethal pain-killing doses of medicine without consent.

In practice, half of those who were no longer physically able to give consent had expressed the wish for euthanasia earlier. Most were in the last stages of disease. But Van der Wal agrees, "It's a weak point in your system if you don't know what the patient really wants. There is always the danger that you are ending life against the will of the patient."

UNDER THE DUTCH HEALTH CARE SYSTEM, THERE IS NO FINANCIAL INCENTIVE TO ABUSE EUTHANASIA

In the Netherlands, the circumstances for allowing physicians to help their patients to die are among the best that can be found at the moment. Due to the nation's commitment to equality in the provision of health care, people are not forced to shorten their lives on economic grounds, and the prevailing respect for liberty and personal autonomy allows people to make their own choices without the undue influence of others. . . .

It is perfectly acceptable that physicians can help their patients to die in the Netherlands, because the social environment supports the arrangement. Instead of wasting their time on criticizing the Dutch situation, bioethicists from other countries should strive to improve their own national health care systems to the point where the autonomy of individuals can be taken fully into account even when they want to hasten their own demise.

Heta Häyry, *Bioethics*, July 1997.

It's a weak point as well that the Dutch laws don't make a distinction between mental and physical suffering. Not long ago, a psychiatrist performed euthanasia on a physically healthy woman who had lost her children and was in deep despair. He was acquitted in a case that left public confidence rattled.

The policy of gedogen doesn't help the Dutch decide what to think of those who value independence so much they want to control their own death. Nor does it help a doctor who carries the burden and power of deciding when someone has suffered "enough."

What is notable is that 71 percent of the Dutch remain firm in their support of euthanasia policies. There is a palpable pride in doing things "the Dutch way." Pride in a system in which the law evolves with public consensus.

GRAPPLING WITH COMPLEXITY INSTEAD OF DENYING IT

Yet time and again, even the strongest supporters of euthanasia told me, as did a retired family doctor, Herbert Cohen: "Euthanasia is not for export." The difference between Holland and America, they say, is universal health care. No one here chooses to die to protect their family finances.

Perhaps what is exportable, though, is the Dutch tolerance for ambiguity. For living in the ethical gray zone, grappling with complexity instead of denying it, keeping open to change.

If there is an American parallel to the Dutch way, it might be a state-by-state experiment, a testing of different rules and experiences with assisted suicide. The truth is that we too want to find a way of dying that is both merciful and careful.

Yet today, in the countryside of canals and gedogen, it's not always easy to find the right words in an American dictionary.

"Those who are selling the culture of
death . . . have chosen as their role
model . . . a country where
physicians dispense with 900 to
1,000 people a year without the
patient's consent."

LEGALIZED EUTHANASIA IN THE
NETHERLANDS HAS HARMED DUTCH
SOCIETY

Terry Golway

In the following viewpoint, Terry Golway argues that the practice of voluntary euthanasia in the Netherlands is misguided and
dangerous. The Dutch have adopted a culture of death, argues
the author, and their euthanasia policies result in the murder of
between nine hundred and one thousand innocent people each
year. Golway believes the Netherlands is an example of why
euthanasia should not be legalized, but he warns that euthanasia
advocates in America are touting the Netherlands as a model of
tolerance and enlightenment. Terry Golway is a columnist for
the Catholic weekly magazine *America*.

As you read, consider the following questions:
1. How does Goodman, as quoted by Golway, describe the
   discovery that between nine hundred and one thousand
   people per year in the Netherlands die from "involuntary
   euthanasia"?
2. In Golway's opinion, what is the phrase "performed
   euthanasia" a euphemism for?
3. In what way does the author feel that euthanasia is similar to
   capital punishment?

Reprinted from Terry Golway, "Life in the 90's," *America*, May 10, 1997, by permission of
America Press, Inc; ©1997. All rights reserved.

There are times, friends, when those who hold human life to be sacred seem as exotic and old-fashioned as the Amish farmers of Lancaster County, Pa. There are days when it is possible to envision a time in the not very distant future when people in short pants and sneakers, with cameras hanging from their necks, will gawk at sturdy, God-fearing, life-affirming folk and wonder in amazement that such people could exist in the modern world.

THE "ENLIGHTENED" DUTCH

The morning newspaper has brought a dispatch from the Netherlands about the joys of euthanasia. It was ever so earnest—why, there wasn't even an attempt at cheap irony: A country called the Netherlands has become the international capital of euthanasia, the place to be if you're in pain (or perhaps even if you're not) and you wish (or maybe you don't) to be dispatched to the netherworld.

The writer, the syndicated columnist Ellen Goodman, made predictably reasonable arguments on behalf of needle-wielding Dutch doctors. No doubt you will take comfort in knowing that there are layers upon layers of bureaucracy one must hurdle before winning the "right" to die! And the doctors—they are ever so careful about deciding who shall die and who shall not! It is positively uplifting! The Dutch, you see, have been thinking a lot about this business of euthanasia.

Apparently yet another wide-eyed American has been dazzled by the sophistication and the cool rationality of the Old World. "Holland has grappled longer and more publicly with the end-of-life issues that we are only now beginning to confront seriously," the columnist wrote. And, she added, the Dutch bristle when they hear that coarse, unthinking and church-going Americans believe that they are "ridding themselves of the old and the handicapped."

A "TROUBLING DISCOVERY"

Of course they are doing no such thing. They are merely getting rid of people who want to be gotten rid of. For the most part. Nearly always. As in any activity—baseball, omelette-making, euthanasia—there's the occasional error. But why focus on the botched ground ball when you can feast your eyes on a glorious home run!

In the course of this starry-eyed glimpse of the doctors who slip their patients the ultimate mickey, the columnist conceded that, sure, mistakes have been made. "The most troubling discovery is that 900 to 1,000 patients a year die from what they call 'involuntary euthanasia,'" Goodman wrote. In the rational, reasonable world in which a fair number of our cultural and media elites reside, the doctor-assisted killing of 900 to1,000 people a year is merely "troubling." If you want to get the elite really outraged, really motivated, you'll have to do something a bit more hideous. Try proposing vouchers for parents of parochial-school children.

AN ABSURD EUPHEMISM

In what, in another age, would have been the central point of this discussion, the columnist noted in passing that "it's a weak point . . . that the Dutch laws don't make a distinction between mental and physical suffering." Now, are you ready for this year's award for best use of a euphemism by a columnist? Here goes: "Not long ago, a psychiatrist performed euthanasia on a physically healthy woman who had lost her children and was in deep despair."

Reprinted by permission of Chuck Asay and Creators Syndicate.

Performed euthanasia? Back in the old days, we simple folk would have used a less grandiose verb—*murdered*. Ah, but in preparing Americans for that fine day when trained physicians dispose of the unwanted, we mustn't use judgmental language. So, you see, psychiatrists who believe their patients are in deep despair don't kill them. Why, only a coarse American would use such a word. Kindly souls that these Dutch doctors are, they, in their humane way, *perform euthanasia.*

Those who are selling the culture of death as the next century's way of life have chosen as their role model a country in which a psychiatrist can kill you if he or she thinks you're too depressed, a country where physicians dispense with 900 to 1,000 people a year without the patient's consent. Rather than recoil with horror, the merchants of death would like to see America adopt similarly enlightened policies.

It's fair to say that many of the people preparing the way for euthanasia in America, who regard a few "involuntary" cases as sufficient price to pay for a greater "good," are vociferous opponents of capital punishment. But what is capital punishment but the state performing a form of involuntary euthanasia on an unwanted population? Those who treasure the gift of life and who oppose its taking, whether by government or by physician, have a relentless consistency to their arguments. The cultural leftists who support abortion and suicide on demand, but who turn squeamish on the matter of capital punishment, ought to spend some time thinking through their arguments. They might discover, as pro-lifers have said for years, that on matters of life and death, it is a slippery slope indeed.

Resisting the Culture of Death

The matter-of-fact arguments on behalf of the Dutch way of death, the use of the absurd phrase "performed euthanasia" in the work of a well-known syndicated columnist—these are signs that the forces of darkness are gathering.

Those who have a different view of life can take some comfort and draw some succor from the knowledge that the late Cardinal Joseph Bernardin's autobiography remains on the bestseller list. Clearly his example continues to inspire, and his arguments against the culture of death remain cogent, vital and—we can only hope and pray—decisive.

"Once the pain and symptoms of an
illness are under control, people
rarely talk about taking their own
lives."

HOSPICE CARE CAN MAKE ASSISTED SUICIDE UNNECESSARY

Joe Loconte

In the following viewpoint, Joe Loconte contends that hospice
care, not assisted suicide, is the best solution to people's fears
about dying a prolonged, painful death. Despite claims to the
contrary, writes Loconte, most dying patients' suffering can be
controlled, but often is not because doctors are undertrained in
end-of-life care. In the author's opinion, increasing the availability of hospice care would end the movement to legalize assisted
suicide because it would assure people that they will receive attention and care throughout the dying process. Joe Loconte is
deputy editor of the conservative magazine Policy Review, from
which this viewpoint is excerpted.

As you read, consider the following questions:

1. Where are patients under hospice care usually treated?
2. How has Ira Byock responded to Timothy Quill's assertion
   that the physical suffering of the terminally ill cannot always
   be effectively relieved, as quoted by the author?
3. What is the "larger objective" of hospice care, as phrased by
   Loconte?

Excerpted from Joe Loconte, "Hospice, Not Hemlock," Policy Review, March/April 1998.
Reprinted with permission from Policy Review, a publication of the Heritage Foundation.

In the deepening debate over assisted suicide, almost everyone agrees on a few troubling facts: Most people with terminal illnesses die in the sterile settings of hospitals or nursing homes, often in prolonged, uncontrolled pain; physicians typically fail to manage their patients' symptoms, adding mightily to their suffering; the wishes of patients are ignored as they are subjected to intrusive, often futile, medical interventions; and aggressive end-of-life care often bankrupts families that are already in crisis.

Too many people in America are dying a bad death.

The solution, some tell us, is physician-assisted suicide. Oregon has legalized the practice for the terminally ill. Michigan's Jack Kevorkian continues to help willing patients end their own lives. The prestigious *New England Journal of Medicine* has come out in favor of doctor-assisted death. Says Faye Girsh, the director of the Hemlock Society: "The only way to achieve a quick and painless and certain death is through medications that only a physician has access to."

A BETTER WAY TO DIE

This, we are told, is death with dignity. What we do not often hear is that there is another way to die—under the care of a specialized discipline of medicine that manages the pain of deadly diseases, keeps patients comfortable yet awake and alert, and surrounds the dying with emotional and spiritual support. Every year, roughly 450,000 people die in this way. They die in hospice.

"The vast majority of terminally ill patients can have freedom from pain and clarity of mind," says Martha Twaddle, a leading hospice physician and medical director at the hospice division of the Palliative CareCenter of the North Shore, in Evanston, Illinois. "Hospice care helps liberate patients from the afflictions of their symptoms so that they can truly live until they die."

The hospice concept rejects decisions to hasten death, but also extreme medical efforts to prolong life for the terminally ill. Rather, it aggressively treats the symptoms of disease—pain, fatigue, disorientation, depression—to ease the emotional suffering of those near death. It applies "palliative medicine," a team-based philosophy of caregiving that unites the medical know-how of doctors and nurses with the practical and emotional support of social workers, volunteer aides, and spiritual counselors. Because the goal of hospice is comfort, not cure, patients are usually treated at home, where most say they would prefer to die.

"Most people nowadays see two options: A mechanized, depersonalized, and painful death in a hospital or a swift death that rejects medical institutions and technology," says Nicholas Christakis, an assistant professor of medicine and sociology at the University of Chicago. "It is a false choice. Hospice offers a way out of this dilemma."

HOSPICE OR HEMLOCK?

If so, there remains a gauntlet of cultural roadblocks. Hospice is rarely mentioned in medical school curricula. Says Dale Smith, a former head of the American Academy of Hospice and Palliative Medicine, "Talk to any physician and he'll tell you he never got any training in ways to deal with patients at the end of life."

The result: Most terminally ill patients either never hear about the hospice option or enter a program on the brink of death. Though a recent Gallup Poll shows that nine out of 10 Americans would choose to die at home once they are diagnosed with a terminal disease, most spend their final days in hospitals or nursing homes.

And, too often, that's not a very good place to die. A four-year research project funded by the Robert Wood Johnson Foundation looked at more than 9,000 seriously ill patients in five major teaching hospitals. Considered one of the most important studies on medical care for the dying, it found that doctors routinely subject patients to futile treatment, ignore their specific instructions for care, and allow them to die in needless pain.

"We are failing in our responsibility to provide humane care for people who are dying," says Ira Byock, a leading hospice physician and the author of Dying Well. George Annas, the director of the Law, Medicine and Ethics Program at Boston University, puts it even more starkly: "If dying patients want to retain some control over their dying process, they must get out of the hospital."

That's precisely the argument that hospice advocates have been making for the last 25 years. Hospice programs are, in fact, the only institution in the country with a record of compassionate, end-of-life care for people with incurable illnesses. The hospice movement, and the palliative approach to medicine it represents, could revolutionize America's culture of dying.

Since the mid-1970s, hospice programs have grown from a mere handful to more than 2,500, available in nearly every community. At least 4,000 nurses are now nationally certified in hospice techniques. In Michigan—Kevorkian's home state—a statewide hospice program cares for 1,100 people a day, regardless of their ability to pay. The Robert Wood Johnson Foundation, a leading health-care philanthropy, has launched a $12-

million initiative to improve care for the dying. And the American Medical Association, which did not even recognize hospice as a medical discipline until 1995, has made the training of physicians in end-of-life care one of its top priorities.

There is a conflict raging in America today over society's obligations to care for its most vulnerable. Says Charles von Gunten, a hospice specialist at Northwestern Memorial Hospital, in Chicago, "It is fundamentally an argument about the soul of medicine." One observer calls it a choice between hospice or hemlock—between a compassion that "suffers with" the dying, or one that eliminates suffering by eliminating the sufferer. . . .

REDEFINING AUTONOMY

The starting place for any hospice team is the patient: What kind of care does he or she really want? "It's not about our goals for a patient," says Dorothy Pitner, the president of the Palliative Care-Center of the North Shore, which cares for about 200 people a day in Chicago's northern suburbs. "They tell us how they define quality of life, and then together we decide the course of action."

This is how hospice respects patient autonomy: not by hastening death, but by working closely with patients and families to weigh the costs and benefits of care. "Patients have the right to refuse unwanted, futile medical care," says Walter Hunter, the chairman of the National Hospice Ethics Committee. "But the right to refuse care does not mean the right to demand active assistance in dying." Patients resolve the tradeoffs between controlling pain and feeling alert; they choose whether to use a medical device that provides them with nutrients but causes swelling and congestion. . . .

THE IMPORTANCE OF RELIEVING PAIN

Interviews with hospice caregivers uncover a singular experience: Once the pain and symptoms of an illness are under control, people rarely talk about taking their own lives. "Those requests go away with good palliative care," says von Gunten, who directs palliative education at Northwestern University Medical School. "I see this on a routine basis."

The Hospice of the Florida Suncoast, in operation since 1977, works mostly with retirees in Pinellas County. Now the largest community-based hospice in the country, it has about 1,200 patients under care on any given day. Programs extend to nearly all of the 100 or so nursing homes in the area. About 80 percent of all county residents with end-stage cancer find their way into its orbit of care.

Hospice president Mary Labyak says many people come in eager to hasten their own deaths, but almost always have a change of heart. Of the 50,000 patients who have died under the group's care, she says, perhaps six have committed suicide. "The public perception is that people are [choosing suicide] every day. But these are people in their own homes, they have the means, they have lots of medication, and they don't choose death."

Hardly anything creates a more frightening sense of chaos than unrelieved pain and suffering. "We know that severe pain greatly reduces people's ability to function," says Patricia Berry, the director of the Wisconsin Cancer Pain Initiative. "If we don't control symptoms, then people can't have quality of life, they can't choose what they want to do or what to think about."

A RIGHT TO HOSPICE CARE

I submit that the answer to the problem of assisted suicide lies not in more euthanasia but in more hospice care. The first order of business should be to establish that dying patients have a constitutional right to competent hospice care. Only *after* this right has been established does it make sense for the courts to turn their attention to the question of whether terminally ill patients should have an additional constitutional right to physician-assisted euthanasia.

M. Scott Peck, *Newsweek*, March 10, 1997.

By interrupting sleep, curbing appetite, and discouraging personal interactions, pain doesn't just aggravate a person's physical condition. It also leads, as a recent report by the Institute of Medicine puts it, to "depression and demoralization" of the sufferer. Says David English, the president of the Hospice of Northern Virginia, one of the nation's oldest programs, "You can't address the psychosocial issues of a person who is in pain."

Hospice has understood this connection between pain and overall well-being from the start. After conventional treatments fail, says Martha Twaddle, "you'll often hear doctors say 'there's nothing left to do.' There's a lot left to do. There is a lot of aggressive care that can be given to you to treat your symptoms.". . .

SUFFERING CAN ALWAYS BE ALLEVIATED

The pain-control approach of hospice depends on an aggressive use of opioid drugs—narcotics such as morphine, fentanyl, codeine, or methadone. Despite the effectiveness of these drugs in clinical settings, euthanasia supporters often ignore or contest the results. Timothy Quill, a leading advocate of doctor-assisted suicide, writes that "there is no empirical evidence that all physical suffering associated with incurable illness can be effectively relieved."

Ira Byock, the president of the American Academy of Hospice and Palliative Medicine, says that's medical bunk. A 20-year hospice physician, Byock has cared for thousands of patients with terminal disease. "The best hospice and palliative-care programs have demonstrated that pain and physical suffering can always be alleviated," he says. "Not necessarily eliminated, but it can always be lessened and made more tolerable."

Physicians and other authorities outside the hospice movement agree that most pain can be controlled. Authors of the New York Task Force report assert that "modern pain relief techniques can alleviate pain in all but extremely rare cases." A primer on cancer-pain management from the U.S. Department of Health and Human Services (HHS) urges clinicians to "reassure patients and families that most pain can be relieved safely and effectively.". . .

When people are not in pain, they eat better and their body's immune system often improves. They usually become more mobile, decreasing their risk of respiratory infection. At least for a time, these patients rebound, and many go on to live weeks longer than anyone anticipated. Hospice nurses and social workers say they see this occur all the time.

TREATING THE WHOLE PATIENT

Not long ago oncology staff from Evanston Hospital, counseled in pain control techniques by Martha Twaddle, called her to report that a patient with prostate cancer who received morphine was barely breathing. Twaddle decided to visit the man herself.

"What is it that hurts?" she asks.

The man mumbles something about a machine.

Twaddle eventually understood: The patient is an octogenarian Russian immigrant who doesn't understand much English. "He had experienced the Holocaust, and now they're taking him down every day to a machine for radiation. So when they put him on the gurney, he says he's in pain."

She shakes her head. "You don't treat anxiety and fear with morphine. You treat anxiety and fear with education and support."

This is what hospice staff mean by holistic or palliative medicine: Their medical gaze sees beyond the disease itself. Though important, the hospice contribution to pain management represents only part of its strategy of care. Its support for palliative medicine may prove to be the movement's most important legacy.

A DEBT TO HOSPICE

Palliative care studies are now appearing at major universities, hospitals, and research centers. The United Hospital Fund in New York City has organized a 12-hospital project to test palliative care programs. D.C.'s George Washington University researchers have set up a Center to Improve Care of the Dying. The federal Assisted Suicide Funding Restriction Act, passed last year, authorizes HHS to fund research projects that emphasize palliative medicine to improve care for the terminally ill.

Oddly enough, until the doctor-assisted suicide debate, the hospice philosophy of care was not acknowledged by the medical establishment. The nation's top medical schools, the American Medical Association, the College of Physicians, the Institute of Medicine, and the National Academy of Science all mostly ignored the movement and its aims.

"They all acted as if hospice was a friendly aunt who would sit and hold the hand of a patient, but not anything serious adults needed to pay attention to," Byock says. "But now hospice is being recognized as a robust, medically competent, team-based approach to the person and family who are confronting life's end.". . .

LIVING UNTIL THEY DIE

Even the goal of easing people's suffering, as central as it is to hospice care, is not an end in itself. The aim of comfort is part of a larger objective: to help the terminally ill live as fully as possible until they die. This is where hospice departs most pointedly both from traditional medicine and the advocates of assisted suicide.

Hospice, by shining a light on the emotional and spiritual aspects of suffering, is challenging the medical community to reexamine its priorities. The period at the end of life, simultaneously ignored and micromanaged by conventional approaches, can be filled with significance. To neglect it is to diminish ourselves. "Spiritual inattentiveness in the face of dying and death can lead to the sad spectacle of medical technology run amok," says Laurence O'Connell, the president of the Park Ridge Center, a medical ethics think tank in Chicago.

Those who have spent years tending to the dying say there is a mystery at life's end, one that seems to defy the rules of medicine. Walter Hunter, a medical director at the Hospice of Michigan, recalls a patient with end-stage kidney disease who entered hospice and quickly asked to be taken off of the hemo-dialysis (a kidney machine) needed to keep her alive. Conventional medical wisdom put her life expectancy at two to three weeks without the technology, but the woman said she was eager to die.

Eight months later she was still alive. She asked Hunter, then her primary doctor, why she was still breathing. "I don't know," the doctor replied. "According to the textbooks, you should be dead."

Hospice staff had been busy in those months, keeping the patient comfortable, providing emotional and spiritual support. They later learned that just two days before the woman died, she had reconciled with one of her estranged children.

Sharon McCarthy has been a social worker at the Palliative CareCenter of the North Shore for 18 years. She has cared for thousands of dying patients, getting a ringside seat to the grief of countless families. For the vast majority, she says, hospice provides the window of opportunity to get their lives in order. One of the most common desires: forgiveness, both extended and received. "There's a lot of non-physical pain that goes on when these things aren't done." Says Mary Sheehan, director of clinical services and a 12-year veteran in hospice: "Ninety-nine percent of the time they have unfinished business."

SAVING THE SOUL OF MEDICINE

Hospice or hemlock: Though both end in death, each pursues its vision of a "good death" along radically different paths. At its deepest level, the hospice philosophy strikes a blow at the notion of the isolated individual. It insists that no one dies in a vacuum. Where one exists, hospice physicians, nurses, and social workers rush in to help fill it.

For many hospice staff and supporters, such work is motivated and informed by a deeply moral and religious outlook. "I do not work within a specific religious context," writes Byock in Dying Well, "but I find more than a little truth in the spiritual philosophies of Christianity, Buddhism, and Judaism." Karen Bell, the hospice director of the Catholic-run Providence Health System in Portland, Oregon, says her organization is propelled by religious values. "The foundational principle is that life has a meaning and value until the very end, regardless of a person's physical condition or mental state."

Faith communities have always been involved in caring for the desperately ill, founding hospitals, clinics, medical schools, and so on. Though not usually connected to religious institutions, nearly all hospice programs make spiritual counseling available; rabbis, chaplains, and ecumenical ministers make frequent home visits and regularly attend hospice team meetings.

For many religious physicians, tackling the issue of personal autonomy is a crucial step in end-of-life care. "This is the Christian answer to whose life it is: 'It is not your own; you were bought at a price,'" says Yale University Medical School's Dr. Diane Komp, quoting the apostle Paul. "But if we are not in control of our lives, then we need companionship. We need the companionship of God and the companionship of those who reflect the image of God in this broken world."

Leon Kass, a physician and philosopher at the University of Chicago, says the religiously inspired moral vigor of hospice sets itself squarely against the movement for assisted death. "Hospice borrows its energy from a certain Judeo-Christian view of our obligations to suffering humanity," he says. "It is the idea that company and care, rather than attempts at cure, are abiding human obligations. These obligations are put to the severest test when the recipient of care is at his lowest and most unattractive."

We seem, as a culture, to be under such a test, and the outcome is not at all certain. Some call it a war for the soul of medicine. If so, hospice personnel could be to medical care what American GIs were to the Allied effort in Europe—the source of both its tactical and moral strength and, eventually, the foot soldiers for victory and reconstruction.

| "Physician-assisted death is a narrow question to be raised only when good palliative care fails."

DYING PATIENTS SHOULD HAVE ACCESS TO BOTH HOSPICE CARE AND ASSISTED SUICIDE

Timothy E. Quill

In the following viewpoint, Timothy E. Quill, a professor of medicine at the University of Rochester in New York, argues that dying patients should have access to physician-assisted death when hospice care fails. Hospice care can be extremely effective, he maintains, but it cannot always relieve a patient's suffering. Quill believes that in these rare instances when hospice care fails, doctors and patients should be able to discuss assisted suicide without fear of legal sanction. The author acknowledges some of potential dangers of legalizing assisted suicide, but also contends that current prohibitions on euthanasia cause doctors to ignore the suffering endured by terminally ill persons.

As you read, consider the following questions:
1. What is hospice care's foremost value to the patient, in Quill's opinion?
2. Why does Quill feel that the term "suicide" is inappropriate when applied to a terminally ill person's request for assistance in dying?
3. Legally, what is a doctor's safest reply to a patient who requests assistance in dying, as phrased by the author?

Reprinted from Timothy E. Quill, "Deciding About Death: Physician-Assisted Suicide and the Courts: A Panel Discussion," Pharos, Winter 1998, vol. 61, no. 1, by permission of Pharos. Copyright ©1998 by Alpha Omega Alpha Honor Medical Society.

B ecause it is hard to address the legal and constitutional issues surrounding physician-assisted dying without having
some feel for the background clinical and ethical issues, I will
begin there. I am a primary care doctor. I am also a hospice doctor. I love the work that I do. And when we use medicine's technology to keep people alive and functioning, even into their
nineties, we are doing wondrous work.

But we all know that growing old and getting sick aren't for
sissies. Sometimes the very interventions we use to keep people
alive longer indirectly prolong their dying. Even where there is
much suffering, dying people can find moments of meaning
and connection, extraordinary moments to be cherished. And
when we can help people achieve a peaceful, calm death, the
kind of death we would all like to have, we are doing a wondrous task. This goal should be part of medicine, part of our
professional responsibility. But it is not easy: sometimes, dying
is filled with medical interventions, many with harsh, unintended consequences, so that people can end up in very hard
situations. Physicians have a responsibility to respond to these
hard situations, just as we have a responsibility to help our patients experience the good situations.

THE IMPORTANCE OF HOSPICE CARE

With [hospice advocate] Elisabeth Kübler-Ross as our symbolic
guide, I shall talk first about the hospice or palliative care values
that should drive this debate. In acute-care medicine, prolonging life is often our foremost objective, and we ask people to
endure considerable suffering in the interest of potential recovery and a return to a meaningful life. You would never ask
someone to endure an intensive care unit or harsh chemotherapy unless it were for a higher purpose. In hospice care, we acknowledge that we cannot affect the outcome of the disease or
prolong life as we would wish, so we make relief of suffering
through aggressive symptom management our highest priority.
Fundamental to hospice care is getting to know the person as a
unique individual and trying to respond to his or her situation
using his or her own values. We want to give this individual all
possible choice and control, recognizing, of course, that he or
she does not have his or her preferred choices. To a person, all
hospice patients would choose to get better or return to meaningful life, if that were in their repertoire.

Hospice care's foremost value to the patient may be nonabandonment. We commit to going through the dying process with
the patient, wherever this leads. Whether it takes us to places

where palliative care instructs us, or to a place where there are no landmarks, where no one knows what to do, we will go there, regardless. In the latter scenario, we will be with the patient and try to problem-solve. Conversing about physician assistance in dying is reserved for cases in which we have gone through this process with the patient, and in which the patient's end-stage suffering is extreme and intolerable—death is all that awaits.

REAL HUMAN EXPERIENCE VERSUS ETHICAL THEORY

One way I have participated in this policy debate is by telling stories of real people, stories that point up a tension between real human experience and the law, between clinical practice realities and principled ethics. Let me tell you a story, then. A young woman, a graduate student in religion and psychology and a practicing Buddhist, developed abdominal pain while working on her thesis. In three brief days, she went from worrying that she might have an ulcer to hoping she had a lymphoma—because lymphoma is treatable—to knowing she was dying of gastric cancer. She was offered hospice care because chemotherapy does not work for gastric cancer. But she felt abandoned, and went in desperate search of ways to fight this illness. This is when she became my patient.

Together, she and I explored all options, and she elected to try experimental treatment because, at least, that had *not* been shown *not* to work. But she wanted reassurance that she could stop if the going got too hard. That was easy, ethically and legally: people can choose to stop treatment once we are sure they know what they are giving up. She also wanted to know that, if her dying got to be very bad at the end, I would not let her linger and die an agonizing death. For a practicing Buddhist, how you die—your psychological and spiritual state as you depart this life—has important bearing on how you are reborn in the next. This patient wanted me to help her through her dying, wherever it went. To make such a commitment is hard, because our society draws some sharp distinctions between ways physicians can and cannot help people. But I made that commitment to her, as I do to all of my patients who are dying. Thus reassured, she undertook experimental therapy, surgery, and radiation. None, however, worked very well.

After a month in the hospital, experiencing these interventions, this patient turned to hospice, and, under hospice care, went home to prepare to die. She elected to keep her central line in place because, with no stomach, she could not eat. Her pain was well controlled with morphine infusion. She had a wonderful month: she married her long-time boyfriend; her Buddhist community came to the hospital twice weekly for group meditation in which everyone was invited to participate; she gave away her favorite possessions as mementos. After a month, her symptoms intensified, her pain reaching a level where the medicines to control it would also cloud her consciousness. For a Buddhist, clouded consciousness is not a good thing. She also had intractable nausea and vomiting and an open abdominal wound that was foul-smelling and, to her, humiliating. She was ready to die.

A LAST RESORT

She knew from our conversations that she had some options. She could discontinue her central line, which supplied fluids. She could accept the sedation that comes with higher doses of pain medicine. After a conversation to make sure she understood her choices, the latter was the way she died over the ensuing four or five days. Her death—a good death—occurred in the course of standard hospice care, using hospice values. But it also involved an explicit decision around ending life. The current national policy debate focuses on methods of response to such explicit decisions. To me, the process of physician and patient working together collaboratively over time is much more important than the specific method whereby death is eased.

Physician-assisted death is a narrow question to be raised only when good palliative care fails. Sometimes palliation fails because we are not doing it well enough. Regardless of where we stand individually in the assisted-death debate, we must work together to remedy the inadequacies in the availability and delivery of good palliative care. We don't teach doctors about palliation as we do about CPR or blood gas analysis. And we tend to offer palliative care very late in an illness, when all else has failed—we must learn to offer it earlier and deliver it longer. We still worry about addiction and overdose with pain medication, and doctors worry about being reviewed; these anxieties lead us to undermedicate dying persons. And we have enormous healthcare access problems in this country, to hospice care in particular. We would never want assisted dying to be an alternative to the best care we can deliver. Finally, we must be very aware of how reimbursement incentives might influence our choices.

HOSPICE CARE HAS LIMITS

But there are inherent limitations to hospice care. We are good at relieving suffering on hospice, but not 100 percent of the time. We must learn to acknowledge the exceptions. If we cannot talk about this, our patients think we shall not face up to the extreme suffering if they are so unlucky as to experience it. Sometimes this suffering arises from uncontrollable physical symptoms. Data about what patients on hospice report about pain relief, or relief of shortness of breath, in the last week of life, are sobering. Despite what doctors and nurses report about achieving good symptom relief for hospice patients in the last week of life, the patients themselves often say that they are still experiencing severe pain and shortness of breath. And, given the psychosocial and spiritual dimensions of suffering, it is unrealistic to expect hospice to relieve all suffering. Finally, the dependency and side effects that people endure over a long dying are simply unacceptable to some. Lying in bed in diapers is an experience outside some people's envelope.

NOT A PANACEA

I applaud the promotion of hospice care in the media. Promoting compassionate palliative care to the general public is essential, especially if one believes that physician-assisted suicide should be made available in the context of offering choices. . . .

The problem with hospice care, however, is that in spite of our best public relations efforts, it doesn't always take away people's pain, and it isn't always wanted. . . .

Dressing up hospice care as a panacea, and the only moral alternative to physician-assisted suicide is unhelpful, and inaccurate. . . .

Hospice care is wonderful for some. Physician-assisted suicide is a valid choice for others.

John L. Miller, *American Journal of Hospice and Palliative Care*, May/June 1997.

We regularly make life-ending decisions in the hospital. We allow people to stop life-sustaining treatment. We handle this process out in the open by putting our best minds together and making a forthright decision. As in the case I described, we often use escalating doses of opioids at the very end when the patient agrees to accept sedation in exchange for better pain control. This is a middle ground, some edges of which are now being explored. Terminal sedation offers the patient the option to be heavily sedated and then "allowed to die." This is not euthanasia—we are not assisting in a death but, rather, relieving suffering; the patient dies from dehydration or other problems. Allowing people to stop eating and drinking when they want to die is also being explored. People are desperate for some choice consistent with their own values, and these may be creative, allowable options. Finally, we have the question of physician-assisted suicide now under debate in the United States; voluntary active euthanasia is not presently an issue here.

A note about terminology: *suicide* is not the right word to use in these conversations; it is correct technically but incorrect from a *meaning* point of view. *Suicide*, or self-killing, has as a connotation destruction of the self. People requesting a doctor's assistance in dying feel that their personhood, their very self, is being destroyed by their illness. They see death not as self-destruction but, rather, as salvation or as a way of asserting their remaining personhood.

SANCTIONING ASSISTED DEATH HAS ITS RISKS

What are the risks in changing public policy? There is no risk-free way to proceed. First, sanctioning physician-assisted death might be okay for exceptional cases, such as those I have written about. Most people, unless their religious convictions deem it unacceptable under any and all circumstances, can admit exceptional cases. But if we allow this act to occur in the open, we have to wonder about ordinary practice—ordinary doctors and ordinary patients. Can all of them make these difficult, nuanced decisions? There are many slippery slopes to worry about, but to me the most important is that from voluntary to involuntary. Assisted dying might be a choice that people can make for themselves in real time, but it should not be an option where patients have lost decisional ability and depend on others to choose for them. We still must address the suffering of incapacitated patients, but this is not the way. Sanctioning physician-assisted suicide could lead to subtle or explicit coercion—would there evolve a "duty to die"? And the United States has problems of access to health care in general and to hospice care in particular. It would be obscene if physician-assisted suicide became an option for persons without access to care. Finally, some people worry that this practice would give physicians even more power.

The risks of the current prohibitions deserve careful attention. We fail to acknowledge suffering, which many of our patients have known and seen in their own lives. One bad death affects all who witness it, becoming part of their personal story and one of the places they go when they themselves get sick. If we cannot deal with intractable suffering or pretend it never happens, it becomes very frightening to a be a patient.

The cases I have written about reflect a deeper problem: people are afraid of dying badly. And, when you look at the phenomenology of dying, even on hospice, suffering is more complex and challenging than we acknowledge.

CURRENT PROHIBITIONS MAKE MATTERS WORSE

We also know about a secret practice. In Washington State in a recent year, 16 percent of physicians were explicitly asked to assist somehow in a patient's death; a quarter of those doctors provided patients with potentially lethal medication. This phenomenon is not rare, but it occurs without consultation, without open discussion. All the cards are in the physician's hands, and choices depend on the physician's willingness to take risks or the physician's own values and views on the law. I would not want my future hanging on such unpredictable variables. We should look instead to other values. When a person is dying, straight thinking and honest talk should be paramount. The current legal restrictions muddle clear thinking and discourage honesty. We doctors have learned how to hedge our intentions and to act in purposefully ambiguous ways. This is not the way to administer public policy or encourage us to work with our patients in a straightforward way.

Finally, there is aloneness and abandonment at death. Legally, the physician's safest course is to tell a patient seeking medical assistance in dying, "It's illegal. Doctors don't do this. The AMA says we don't do this. You're on your own." This leaves the patient and family to find their own solution. With a change in public policy, we could create a system—guided by hospice principles and values and protected by safeguards and a review process—that would bring this decision-making process into the open.

CHANGING PUBLIC POLICY

How do we do this? Legislatures are one avenue. The New York State legislature, however, has had difficulty deciding relatively simple end-of-life matters, much less deciding complex questions such as those about physician-assisted suicide for competent, terminally ill patients.

Referendum is another route. Washington, Oregon, and California have had referenda. While public opinion polls show that two-thirds to three-quarters of the people favor allowing doctors and patients more leeway, referenda on this issue seem to break at about 50-50. And there are problems inherent in referenda. For example, the way the original initiative is written is what you are stuck with as a statute. The Oregon initiative included a fourteen-day waiting period for all patients requesting assistance in dying. For patients suffering in extremis at death's door, fourteen days seem fourteen lifetimes. For someone further from imminent death, however, the waiting period may be too short. And yet you are stuck—this is how the law was crafted. Referenda are also costly to conduct and often prompt polarizing political advertising.

Constitutional challenge seemed reasonable in both Washington and New York. The cases in the Ninth Circuit and Second Circuit, each involving three doctors and three terminally ill patients, make two different arguments. The first is that people who are terminally ill and suffering at the end of life have a right to request assistance in dying, and their doctors have a right to respond. This is not an absolute right, but if both parties agree, they should be able to respond in the open. The second argument invokes equal protection: we currently allow some people assistance in dying—those on life support are allowed to stop life support—whereas others in the same or worse condition but not on life support do not have this option.

I am not entirely sure that we should have made this constitutional challenge. We are doing our best to figure out ways to respond. But the current legal prohibition sends all the wrong messages to doctors taking care of patients. No matter what the Supreme Court decides, and especially if the justices say that we should not do this, we shall need to figure out how to respond. First, how do we improve palliative care for all terminally ill persons? And second, how do we respond to those for whom palliative care fails? If the court says we cannot allow physician-assisted suicide, then how should we respond to this difficult second group? Turning our backs may be legally okay but it is morally unacceptable.

Periodical Bibliography

The following articles have been selected to supplement the diverse views presented in this chapter. Addresses are provided for periodicals not indexed in the *Readers' Guide to Periodical Literature*, the *Alternative Press Index*, the *Social Sciences Index*, or the *Index to Legal Periodicals and Books*.

Peter V. Admiraal	"Euthanasia in the Netherlands," *Free Inquiry*, Winter 1996/97.
James F. Bresnahan	"Palliative Care or Assisted Suicide?" *America*, March 14, 1998.
William H.A. Carr	"A Right to Die," *Saturday Evening Post*, September/October 1995.
Stephen L. Carter	"Rush to a Lethal Judgement," *New York Times Magazine*, July 21, 1996.
Rand Richards Cooper	"The Dignity of Helplessness: What Sort of Society Would Euthanasia Create?" *Commonweal*, October 25, 1996.
Ronald Dworkin et al.	"Assisted Suicide: The Philosophers' Brief," *New York Review of Books*, March 27, 1997.
Ezekiel Emanuel	"Whose Right to Die?" *Atlantic Monthly*, March 1997.
Ezekiel Emanuel et al.	"The Practice of Euthanasia and Physician-Assisted Suicide in the United States," *JAMA*, August 12, 1998. Available from PO Box 10946, Chicago, IL 60610-0946.
David J. Garrow	"Nine Justices and a Funeral," *George*, June 1997. Available from 30 Montgomery St., Jersey City, NJ 07032.
John Leo	"Good Sense on 'Right to Die,'" *U.S. News & World Report*, July 7, 1997.
Timothy E. Quill et al.	"The Debate over Physician-Assisted Suicide: Empirical Data and Convergent Views," *Annals of Internal Medicine*, April 1, 1998. Available from 190 N. Independence Mall West, Philadelphia, PA 19106-1572 or http://www.acponline.org/journals/annals.
M.L. Tina Stevens	"What *Quinlan* Can Tell Kevorkian About the Right to Die," *Humanist*, March/April 1997.
David Van Biema	"Is There a Right to Die?" *Time*, January 13, 1997.

CHAPTER 3

WOULD LEGALIZING EUTHANASIA LEAD TO INVOLUNTARY KILLING?

CHAPTER PREFACE

Derek Humphry and Mary Clement, in their book *Freedom to Die*, state that the right-to-die movement is primarily a response to what they call "the onslaught of medical technology"—the fear many people have that their death will be unnaturally prolonged by the use of invasive, unwanted medical treatments. Doctors prescribe aggressive end-of-life treatments in order to preserve life, but Humphry and Clement suggest that they may also have an ulterior motive: "Some suggest that certain physicians over-treat their patients out of simple greed. . . . Dead patients generate no income for either the physician or the hospital."

Opponents of euthanasia, however, cite a different trend within the health care industry. Increasingly, Americans receive their medical care through health maintenance organizations, or HMOs. Under this type of managed care health plan, members pay a fixed monthly fee and the plan provides all their health care needs. Critics point out that an HMO's profits are the difference between how much it receives in membership fees and how much it spends on patient care. In short, many claim that rather than overtreating, HMOs profit by spending as little as possible on their patients.

The rise of managed care has exacerbated concerns that legalized euthanasia might be abused. The International Anti-Euthanasia Task Force sums up these fears: "The cost effectiveness of hastened death is undeniable. The earlier a patient dies, the less costly is his or her care." Critics fear that doctors, hospitals, and insurers will have a financial incentive to pressure dying patients into choosing an early death.

Still, some observers welcome the spread of HMOs and their rejection of the belief that more care is always better. In this view, HMOs are an improvement over the traditional doctor-patient relationship, in which it is most profitable for the physician to keep a patient alive at all costs. Barbara Coombs-Lee, a nurse and right-to-die activist, believes the rise of managed care "should be viewed with relief, as the injection of some modicum of balance in the determination of rational [end-of-life] treatment plans."

Advocates on both sides of the issue acknowledge that the various financial incentives within the health care system can influence both doctors' and patients' decisions regarding end-of-life care and euthanasia. The authors in the following chapter consider these and other factors, and debate whether voluntary euthanasia, if legalized, would be abused.

"In a secular society, driven
exclusively by utilitarian
considerations, to proceed from
physician-assisted suicides to wholly
involuntary killings of patients is a
matter of inescapable logic."

LEGALIZING EUTHANASIA WOULD LEAD TO INVOLUNTARY KILLING

James Thornton

James Thornton is a Roman Catholic priest and a contributor to
the *New American*, a magazine published by the constitutionalist
organization the John Birch Society. In the following viewpoint,
he argues that if physician-assisted suicide becomes legal, it will
inevitably be used by the government to eliminate individuals
whose lives society deems burdensome or without value. Thornton describes Nazi Germany and the Netherlands as examples of
places where euthanasia has been abused. He warns that the
United Sates is on a similar track, citing the acceptance of abortion as evidence that Americans are already willing to destroy
life when it becomes inconvenient to others.

As you read, consider the following questions:
1. Why was a euthanasia program initially begun in Nazi
   Germany, according to Thornton?
2. In the author's view, when did the U.S. government first
   begin to deny the sacredness of human life?
3. In the Netherlands, what categories of patients—besides the
   terminally ill—has euthanasia been extended to, according to
   Thornton?

Excerpted from James Thornton, "Defying the Death Ethic," *The New American*, May 26,
1997, with permission from *The New American*.

One of the symptoms of a society in the grips of moral crisis is a tendency to refer to reprehensible acts by soft-sounding euphemisms, by names that do not directly excite human qualms or agitate scruples and that evade precise reflection on the reality of certain situations. For example, in our modern lexicon, abortion is called "freedom of choice," sexual libertinage is dubbed "alternative lifestyles," and certain forms of genocide-in-slow-motion can be made to seem more acceptable under the name "family planning."

Such are the mental tricks and the "word magic" employed to quiet the normal functioning of our consciences. Sadly, they work on a great many people for long periods of time. Like certain narcotics, they dull the moral senses and can eventually blot out such feelings completely.

This being so, let us examine a concept that is very old, that disappeared from civilized life for almost two millennia, and that has now begun its return, lifting itself ever higher on the distant horizon, like a huge, menacing, black cloud. That concept is known as euthanasia.

"Good Death"

The English word euthanasia is derived from the Greek and means, literally, "good death." According to its oldest meaning, it signifies merely the relatively painless, gentle passage of someone from this life to the next, without necessarily any human inference or intervention. Even in the Christian tradition, we sometimes hear the term "good death" used in the sense that the departed person died at peace with himself, with his family, and with God.

However, an alternative definition, more in accord with contemporary usages, generally suggests something quite different: It indicates the bringing about of the death of a human being, either by suicide or killing, ostensibly to prevent extreme physical pain or mental anguish. Euthanasia, according to the teaching of every traditional Christian group, is looked upon as suicide or murder, plain and simple, and, until recently, was universally condemned in all societies whose roots grew out of Christianity. This teaching holds that a supposedly worthy end, in this case the termination of pain and suffering, never, according to traditional moral norms, justifies immoral or unethical means.

With the rise of revolutionary ideologies in the late 18th century, Darwinistic philosophies in the following century, and the concomitant decline in fidelity to Christian teaching, especially among educated classes, changes in belief regarding the dignity and value of human life gradually came to be more widely accepted. The full significance of this change in outlook manifested itself sharply for the first time almost 60 years ago, in one of the most cultivated nations of Europe—Germany, the land of Bach, Schiller, Goethe, and Beethoven.

EUTHANASIA IN NAZI GERMANY

Early in September 1939, shortly after the opening shots of what would become the Second World War, Adolf Hitler held an important conference with key legal and medical officials of the Reich government. Hitler had decided that, in view of Germany's desperate need for hospital beds to accommodate war casualties, a euthanasia program must be undertaken. The incurably insane, those suffering advanced cases of senility, and others suffering similar conditions were to be painlessly killed, opening, in that manner, numerous hospital beds for the war wounded.

In response to Hitler's conference, the chief medical officer of Germany in that era, Dr. Leonardo Conti, immediately began a long series of discussions with legal, medical, and psychiatric experts to insure that whatever happened was done in accordance with law. Characteristically, Hitler quickly became impatient at Conti's delays and, finally, arbitrarily dictated a secret decree. That document authorized certain officials to begin at once to "grant those who are by all human standards incurably ill a merciful death." Census forms, seemingly for statistical purposes only, were circulated to doctors requiring that they list data on all persons with certain incurable mental and physical debilities. Secret panels of medical experts were then convened to decide who among the patients would live and who would die. Many thousands, over the next five years, were thus quietly slain. But there is more to the story.

Sometime in the middle of 1941, Clemens August Count von Galen, the Roman Catholic Bishop of Münster, received confidential reports about what was happening. With great courage, in July of that year, the Bishop delivered a dramatic, stinging rebuke to the persons responsible for the euthanasia program, in an open pastoral letter. Some weeks later he initiated private criminal proceedings in the public courts against the parties responsible, who at that time were still unknown to him. This was required, he explained to his flock, by German law. Any German citizen who had knowledge of a gross violation of criminal law was bound by that law to report it, and, if necessary, to take action to bring it to a halt.

Hitler, embarrassed by these shocking disclosures, ordered a halt to the secret euthanasia operation, but the program continued until February 1945. After the war, medical doctors, and others who initiated and took part in this program, were prosecuted and tried before Allied military tribunals, and a number of the more prominent figures were hanged for their complicity in these crimes. Ordinary Americans, and other people of the civilized world, were deeply horrified in those years by the idea of any government sponsoring such ruthless, immoral policies.

It is a profoundly revelatory fact that the wartime German government was forced to keep this terrible program a secret from the German public. Such were the sensibilities of the German people in those years that even a highly authoritarian regime—indeed a police state—dared not allow the public to become aware of what was happening. Its panic over the public disclosures by Bishop von Galen demonstrates that even the Hitler regime, though it exercised total control of the German press, radio, and all other forms of information dissemination, as well as the police and all public education, nonetheless felt constrained by potential outrage from an aroused public.

MORAL BLINDNESS

Americans, in contrast, do not live in a police state—at least not yet. They still pride themselves on their maintenance of a system of self-government, and on an open society with unfettered speech and independent communications. Americans also take justifiable pride in the value they have traditionally placed on human life. Life may be cheap in other places in the world, among other peoples and under other governmental systems, but innocent life has traditionally been held dear, and protected, in America.

That remained true until about 25 years ago and the Supreme Court's *Roe v. Wade* decision. Until that time, the sacredness of innocent human life was shielded by law, but more importantly, it was protected by the innate decency and high moral standards of the American people, by an ethos set squarely on the solid foundation of 2,000 years of Christian teaching.

French historian Alexis de Tocqueville referred to these American attributes when he wrote the following words about the America he visited in the 19th century: "In the United States the sovereign authority is religious . . . there is no country in the world where the Christian religion retains a greater influence over the souls of men than in America, and there can be no greater proof of its usefulness and of its conformity to human nature than that its influence is powerfully felt over the most enlightened and free nation of the earth." So it was, and so it remained until liberalism began to eat away at this wholesome influence.

Some Americans of the 1990s, it would seem, have lost moral direction to such an extent that not only are they not offended by an idea that *did* offend and cause shame to Germans living under the Nazi regime in the 1940s, but they unabashedly lend support to the idea, even in public forums. Curiously, many of the justificatory pretexts and rationalizations expressed so frankly today are essentially identical to those quietly or clandestinely advanced in the Third Reich: that we have limited resources that should be expended on the healthy and not the incurably ill; that the incurably sick are a burden on their families and on society; that it is merciful deliberately to end suffering by active intervention—murder, in other words; that innocent human life is not a gift from God, but a condition or state of being the fitness of which is to be judged by medical or governmental authorities alone, according to strictly pragmatic criteria.

Reprinted by permission of Chuck Asay and Creators Syndicate.

One thin barrier separating events of 60 years ago in Germany from the trends of recent decades is the distinction between voluntary and involuntary euthanasia. Theoretically, the arguments advanced today aim towards the legalization of voluntary euthanasia only—that is, to encouraging the notion that those who suffer physically should be allowed to request assistance from others (usually medical doctors) in destroying themselves. In contrast, the German decree dispensed death primarily to persons incapable of making any such decisions about their condition or of expressing their wishes at all. While we must admit that this is indeed a distinction, it is a very tenuous one.

GOVERNMENT ABUSE OF POWER

British writer and philosopher G.K. Chesterton wrote decades ago that the proponents of euthanasia always begin first by seeking the death of those who are nuisances to themselves, but inevitably move on to the next step, seeking death for those who are nuisances to others, once the first step becomes customary. Let us remember that in a bloated, bureaucratic welfare state such as ours, where the government assumes a rapidly expanding role in our lives, where the moral standards have fallen, and where shrinking resources are stretched ever tighter to cover perpetually expanding commitments, it is never long before government is forced to make life and death decisions about "useless eaters" whose cost of care, in dollars and cents, is quite high.

Anyone who surveys the expansion of government power over the past 40 or 50 years cannot doubt that this is true. Whenever government has stepped into some facet of our lives, assurances have poured forth that we citizens need not be concerned, that no expansion of power is contemplated, and that some benefit or largess will be granted free of strings and without any obnoxious controls. Beneficence is always the illusory motive, the grabbing of power and the promotion of evil always the end products.

And of all power, the power over the life or death of innocents is the last one that should ever be willingly entrusted to government. Our own government usurped some of those powers with the Supreme Court decision on abortion nearly 25 years ago. Yet if liberals and other champions of big government have their way, that power will be vastly augmented not by the will of the people or of their elected representatives, but by means of another High Court decision.

On January 8, 1997, the Supreme Court of the United States heard oral arguments for and against the existence of a constitutionally guaranteed right of citizens to choose euthanasia, or physician-assisted suicide. This case, generated in part by years of media publicity about people suffering unbearable pain during terminal illnesses, points to the possibility of a landmark decision, one of those decisive turning points for the whole nation, as significant as the rulings about separation of church and state in the '40s, civil rights in the '50s and '60s, and abortion in the '70s. Like those baneful edicts of past years, this latest one, should it come to pass, will herald a dramatic new chapter in American history, one that further, and calamitously, devaluates life, and that opens new possibilities for government intrusion into the most intimate aspects of our lives. These possibilities frighten many people, most especially persons who are suffering various debilitating diseases and injuries and who, despite their difficulties, do not want to die.

"WITHOUT EXPLICIT REQUEST"

Charles Odom, a 34-year-old resident of Mississippi and former Air Force officer, was injured in an automobile accident in 1984. He remained in a coma for three months after the accident and to this day is severely disabled, requiring the use of a wheelchair to move about. Though his condition may seem daunting to less intrepid men, Odom remains fiercely independent of outside help. Charles Odom traveled all the way from his home to the nation's capital to demonstrate with other disabled people in front of the Supreme Court building. His blunt statement to the press about the Supreme Court deliberations is eloquent in its simplicity: "The worry is that if there's a right to assisted suicide, it will be used to get rid of us." It is easy to imagine bureaucrats and politicians scoffing at this fear, but a quick look at reality shows that it is by no means groundless.

First, as we have seen, what Mr. Odom speaks of is precisely what has happened in other countries at other times. But we need not go back 60 years to Nazi Germany to find a chilling example. Current practices in the Netherlands are enough to give pause to any sensible man or woman. Years ago, the Netherlands changed its laws to permit euthanasia in certain circumstances. At first, physician-assisted suicide for people terminally ill was all that was allowed. Quickly, it was extended to the chronically ill, then to those with psychological afflictions, and finally to those unable to make such decisions at all. In the cold euphemism of the Dutch medical profession, the last category is known as "termination of the patient without explicit request" (suggesting dishonestly, perhaps, that the patient had somehow implicitly requested it). It is documented that each year Dutch doctors actively cause or hasten the deaths of 1,000 patients without the patients' requests. Guidelines and safeguards set down by the Dutch government to regulate euthanasia are routinely ignored, without serious repercussions to the perpetrators.

So, it seems, Charles Odom's fears are definitely not without foundation. In a secular society, driven exclusively by utilitarian considerations, to proceed from physician-assisted suicides to wholly involuntary killings of patients is a matter of inescapable logic, as soon as certain underlying premises are accepted—namely, that innocent life is not a gift from God and that government and medical authorities may do whatever they like for the "good of society.". . .

PROPAGANDA FOR DEATH

Americans of these final years of the 20th century must soundly reject the twisted propaganda for death—that death can deliver them from pain and inconvenience. Doubtless, it is sometimes troublesome, and financially awkward, for some women to carry tiny children within themselves and to give them that greatest of all gifts that can be given—life. Sadly, some of them therefore shrug their obligation and choose death for their offspring, and millions of helpless innocents die. Likewise, it is bothersome and burdensome for some families to care for elders, for the sick, and for the severely disabled, and soon, they too may choose death for their kin, if our courts and politicians are allowed further to infringe on powers that belong to God alone. Millions more will die.

Ill-conceived and diabolical schemes by elected officials, and unconscionable decisions by arrogant judges at all levels in the federal judiciary, promise to make commerce in death as commonplace as commerce in cabbages. If that should come to pass, then our nation will have taken an irretrievable step on the road to moral catastrophe and its twin companion, political despotism. We must prevent our country from taking so fateful a step at all costs, and we must do so now.

"The slippery slope argument reflects lack of faith in the validity of the democratic system."

LEGALIZING EUTHANASIA WOULD NOT LEAD TO INVOLUNTARY KILLING

Gerald A. Larue

Gerald A. Larue is a professor of religion at the University of Southern California in Los Angeles and the author of several books, including *Playing God: 50 Religions' Views on Your Right to Die*, from which the following viewpoint was excerpted. In it, he argues that legalized euthanasia would not be abused by the government because the American people would not allow it. In a democracy, Larue maintains, individuals are free to speak out against unjust practices, and leaders who abuse their power can be removed from office. Therefore, writes the author, claims that euthanasia will inevitably be abused the same way it was in Nazi Germany are unfounded, since that nation under Hitler was not a democracy, and the euthanasia practiced then was never voluntary.

As you read, consider the following questions:

1. What does Larue say about the "so-called domino effect"?
2. In the author's opinion, what types of countercontrols are available in a democracy to protest the abuse of authority?
3. Why is Nazi Germany's euthanasia program not an example of the slippery slope, according to Daniel Callahan, as quoted by the author?

From time to time, those who express concern about the potential deleterious effects of legalizing or endorsing medically-assisted voluntary euthanasia warn about the "slippery slope." According to this theory, once medically assisted euthanasia is legalized for the terminally ill who request it, legalized killing of other groups will automatically follow and even become compulsory. These "other groups" would include the physically and mentally handicapped, the elderly, the impoverished, those who depend on welfare for survival and, perhaps, even members of some specific ethnic, racial, political or religious group. Validation of the "slippery slope" argument is supposed to be found in Nazi Germany where, according to this interpretation, a progression of persecution and death-camp killing was apparent.

BE ALWAYS ON GUARD

How does one respond to such warnings? To begin, it is important to be aware of the legal restraints in proposed legislation for physician-assisted euthanasia. Every possible safeguard against abuse has been introduced. At no place within the proposed legislation is there any hint of bias or prejudice against any group of people. What is proposed is voluntary euthanasia, something that never happened in Germany. Before these terrible scenarios are introduced, the proposals for legislation should be examined as indeed, they have been by medical persons, lawyers, clergy and others who have contributed to the wording and who support the concept. Active, voluntary physician-assisted euthanasia is not a nightmarish notion conjured up by some depraved group of people; it is a response to deep concerns for human well-being and human rights. At the same time, it is important to acknowledge the presence of bigots and racists and organized hate groups in America (and elsewhere in the world). Certainly if such people should ever take control of the nation, they could, possibly, initiate a program similar to that enacted in Nazi Germany. The very recognition of the existence of such persons and groups in a free, democratic society in itself should provide some degree of protection against them.

It is imperative that there be continuing education on the constitutional rights of all persons. The laws that permit hate groups to exist are the same laws that protect us from abuse by such organizations. We are a nation under law. Bigots and hate groups are free to be what they are and to express their distasteful ideas. However, under law, they do not have the right to act out their hatred and bigotry by oppressing others or curtailing the freedom of others. Freedom loving people must be always on guard. In the television program "Hate on Trial," hosted by Bill Moyers, white supremist Tom Metzger uttered this chilling warning:

> I have planted my seeds. They're already in the ground. We're embedded now, don't you understand? We're in your colleges. We're in your armies. We're in your police forces. We're in your technical areas. We're in your banks.

If there is danger of a slippery slope in euthanasia, it resides in the virulent thinking of zealots whose proclaimed biases and attitudes threaten the very freedom we cherish.

PROTECT THE VULNERABLE

The slippery slope argument implies that once the right to voluntary medically-assisted euthanasia is legalized, it will become incumbent upon the handicapped, the frail elderly and others to rid society of their presence. They will recognize themselves as societal burdens, no longer contributing to human welfare while demanding from society excessive energy, time and money for their upkeep. The fact is, such an attitude is now present in some segments of our society and, in some cases, it does lead to suicide, not only by the frail and handicapped, but by those who are poverty stricken or too poor to afford the excessive costs of medical treatment. At this point, social restraints become essential. These restraints grow out of religious and social teachings about the value and sanctity of human life, the love of persons for each other, the compassionate response of humans to others in need of help.

It has also been implied by some who argue against legalized euthanasia that the weak, the infirm and the frail elderly will be coerced, persuaded or cajoled into accepting euthanasia. They will be made to feel useless in a society where the work ethic is dominant and where those who do not produce may be viewed as drains on the vitality of society. They will be persuaded that, inasmuch as they serve no further useful social purpose, it is incumbent upon them to die. Perhaps there will always be those few who seek to dismiss the value of human life and who stand willing to rid society of persons they consider to be useless. It is possible to extend the current "no deposit, no return" mentality to humans. There may also be those few who will seek to be rid of some feeble elder whose continuing existence delays the distribution of inheritances. But to allow fear of such persons to be the basis for ignoring the rights of terminally ill persons who may be in pain, or in a vegetative state, to have their wishes to die fulfilled, seems to be unethical and undemocratic. Leon R. Kass, a medical doctor, has commented:

> Everyone—even those in favor of euthanasia—recognizes the possible abuses, among them the coercion of consent and the slide into killing the weak and the unwanted without their consent. To allay these fears, partisans of euthanasia point to the Netherlands, where for over a decade physicians have been practicing mercy killing with the acquiescence, if not the whole-hearted support, of the law and the larger society. If Holland, without doubt a highly civilized, liberal, and humane nation indeed, in World War II a bastion of principled decency against the unspeakable assaults on human life, opts for mercy killing and practices it without abuse we can take heart and proceed gently into that good night. Let us look to the Dutch.

FATALISTIC ASSUMPTIONS

The slippery slope argument rests on fatalistic assumptions. It reflects the belief that the future is inevitable and that we have absolutely no control over private or public destinies. The implications are that the predictions of "the worst possible scenario" are not simply possible or even probable, but are assured. There

---

UNFOUNDED FEARS

We have no reason to believe that granting the terminally ill the right to voluntary, assisted suicide would somehow lead to co-erced deaths. Back when living wills were controversial, opponents made the same dire prediction, insisting that allowing people to refuse "heroic measures" would lead to the virtual collapse of the medical infrastructure as we know it and turn doctors into Nazis. Nothing of the kind has happened.

Recent claims that involuntary deaths have occurred in the Netherlands (where assisted suicide, although not officially legal, is regulated and not prosecuted) are much exaggerated and distorted. Furthermore, the situation in the Netherlands is not comparable to ours in several important aspects. Perhaps the most significant difference is that the Dutch enjoy national health care. To name a few others, the Dutch guidelines require that doctors determine when their patients' suffering has become "unbearable" and do not require that patients be able to request assistance several times before and at the time of death. In any event, due to the rigorous safeguards built into recent proposals in the United States, abuses would be extremely difficult to perpetrate.

Barbara Dority, Humanist, July/August 1997.

---

is no recognition that in a democratic society we have open to us choices concerning the future. The slippery slide into some sort of compulsory euthanasia as opposed to voluntary euthanasia is not part of that preference.

The slippery slope argument reflects lack of faith in the validity of the democratic system, and in the power of our free society to control by law those who would prey upon the weakness of others or force their particular notions on others. It reflects uneasiness about the ethical and moral qualities of modern humans and would seek to limit human compassion and human autonomy by reacting primarily to fears of what might happen. The so-called domino effect does not operate automatically. Because one action is taken, it does not follow that another more drastic step need follow. Our way of life, with its multiple varieties of human responses that enhance human freedom to make personal choices, invalidates the arguments of those people who would forecast doom at every step.

But what of the references to what happened in Nazi Germany? There a socially advanced nation was transformed politically, morally and ethically, almost overnight. Could the slippery slope that some find in that nation's history be a forewarning of what could happen elsewhere?

THE BASIS FOR THE SLIPPERY SLOPE IDEA

There are two generally quoted bases for the idea of the slippery slope in Nazi Germany. The first comes from a guilt statement by Pastor Martin Niemoller, published in the foreword of his book *Exile in the Fatherland*. Niemoller wrote:

> First they came for the Socialists and I did not speak out
>   Because I was not a Socialist.
> Then they came for the trade unionists, and I did not speak out—
>   Because I was not a trade unionist.
> Then they came for the Jews, and I did not speak out—
>   Because I was not a Jew.
> Then they came for me—
>   And there was no one left to speak for me.

The second basis for the slippery slope idea in Nazi Germany comes from the observations of Dr. Leo Alexander, the Austrian-born psychiatrist, who taught medicine at Harvard and Duke Universities. As a consultant at the trials of Nazi war criminals, he was shocked and dismayed by what he learned of the evil practices done under the name of medicine in Nazi Germany. In 1949, he wrote in an article titled "Medical Science Under Dictatorship" in the *New England Journal of Medicine*:

Whatever proportions these crimes finally assumed, it became evident to all who investigated them that they had started from small beginnings. The beginnings at first were merely a subtle shift in emphasis in the basic attitude of physicians. It started with the acceptance of the attitude, basic in the euthanasia movement, that there is such a thing as life not worthy to be lived. This attitude in its early stages concerned itself merely with the severely and chronically sick. Gradually, the sphere of those to be included in this category was enlarged to encompass the socially unproductive, the ideologically unwanted, and finally all non-Germans. But it is important to realize that the infinitely small wedged-in lever from which this entire trend of mind received its impetus was the attitude toward the nonrehabitable sick.

It is most important to recognize two aspects of these important reports. The first is that what took place in Germany occurred under a dictatorship, not in a democratic setting. So long as the ethnic diversity in America provides opportunity for persons of different racial, religious and ethnic backgrounds to live and work together in freedom and in peace, the patterns of Nazi Germany will remain foreign. If America should ever move towards the kind of dictatorship that Hitler brought to Germany, then our accepted standards of ethical and moral behavior may well be scrapped. Meanwhile, within our democracy the progression described by Dr. Alexander cannot take place.

THE NEED FOR COUNTERCONTROLS

The second aspect lies in what B.F. Skinner has called the need for countercontrols. In the essay "Compassion and Ethics in the Care of Retardates," he pointed out that "The trouble arises because those who exert control are subject to little or no countercontrol." Countercontrols serve to curb violent action and remind those to whom authority and power are given that there are limits on what they may or can do. These same countercontrols serve as the social and ethical reminders that help to curb behavior. Our social countercontrols exist in part in the ballot box where we can vote out of office persons who do not properly represent us or who violate the will of the people; and where we can introduce initiatives supported by signatures of thousands of individuals. Our countercontrols include the media in which investigative reporters call our attention to the acts of those who misuse public trust, where letters to the editor and articles and essays inform us and prompt us to respond. Our countercontrols include the right of the public to protest in rallies. In Germany, as the Nazis assumed control of the nation, there were no valid countercontrols. The church was, for the most part, silent or co-operative. Hitler's propaganda machine educated others to his point of view and dissenting voices were outshouted or silenced. Ultimately, the countercontrol had to come from the outside at the cost of millions of lives. In a democratic system of government countercontrols are always present.

Law in a democratic society develops out of the diversity of community. Where there are "bad" laws, the conscience of members of the community move them to disobey those laws or to seek to change them. In Europe, there were those who rebelled against Nazi regulations and who, disregarding their own welfare, gave protection and succor to Jews who would otherwise have been placed in work camps or put to death. In America, the legalized restrictions of African-American rights that grew out of the slavery mentality were finally challenged and changed. The challenges came from members of both the black and the white communities who were appalled at the indignities suffered by Americans simply on the basis of their darker skin pigmentation. Laws that impacted on the role of women began to change when women were granted full citizenship status and given the right to vote in 1920. The embarrassment of the people of the United States over the undemocratic imprisonment of Japanese-Americans during World War II has been publicly acknowledged. Today our democratic culture is still evolving as citizens become aware of limitations placed on women by males in control of business and the work forces. The humane reactions of concerned and aware persons serve as ever-growing counterforces to practices (whether they are legalized or are reflections of unthinking, but nevertheless demeaning, attitudes) that interfere with human rights or that endanger the lives, property and rights of citizens whether they are healthy or ill, rich or poor, old or young.

"STRAIGHT TO THE KILLING"

It is important to note that despite the implications for Nazi Germany embodied in the Alexander statement, there never was "a slippery slope." As Daniel Callahan has noted:

> The Nazi experience is only partially relevant. Theirs was not a move from legal voluntary euthanasia to involuntary killing. They never had the first phase at all, but went straight to the killing.

The so-called "euthanasia" program, first proposed by Hitler in 1935, initially to get rid of the physically arid mentally handicapped, provides an example of "technological barbarism" which can never be linked to present day "good death" (euthanasia) proposals. Hitler's program began on September 1, 1939 with the enactment of his decree called "Order for the Destruction of Lives Which are Unworthy of Being Lived" (*Vernichtung lebensunwerten Lebens*). As the Fuhrer's psychopathic feelings of insecurity grew, the definition of the "unworthy" expanded. Consequently, some who were labeled "the unfit and unworthy" died in concentration camps like the one at Auschwitz where they entered through a gate bearing the deceptive, mocking, cynical promise that "work makes free" (Arbeit Macht Frei). Some, like the Gypsies, were slaughtered because their dark skins threatened Hitler's concept of a racially pure Aryan Germany (estimates range from 70,000 to 500,000 Gypsy deaths). Ultimately more than eleven million persons were killed.

ANTI-SEMITISM PRECEDED EUTHANASIA IN GERMANY

The murderous slaughter of six million Jews was a genocide resulting, in part, from centuries-old suspicion and raw hatred present in German anti-Semitism. In 1543, Martin Luther spelled out his personal hatred of the Jews in a scurrilous pamphlet entitled "On the Jews and Their Lies," which was widely circulated in Germany for centuries right up to and including the time of Hitler. In crude language, Luther described the Jews as gluttonous, lazy people who "fleece us of our money and our goods." It was Luther's policy for dealing with the Jews that "Hitler would carry out in every detail." What was Luther's final solution?

First, to set fire to their synagogues or schools . . .

Second, I advise that their houses also be razed and destroyed.

Third, I advise that all their prayer books and Talmudic writings, in which such adultery, lies, cursing and blasphemy are taught, be taken from them . . .

Fourth, I advise that their Rabbis be forbidden to teach henceforth on pain of loss of life and limb . . .

Fifth, I advise that safe-conduct on the highways be abolished completely for the Jews . . .

Sixth, I advise that . . . all cash and treasure of silver and gold be taken from them . . .

Seventh . . . let whosoever can, throw brimstone and pitch upon them, so much the better . . . and if this be not enough, let them be driven like mad dogs out of the land.

One need only look into the history of the Jews in Europe to see how difficult their life was for centuries before Nazism. At one time Jewish separatism had been encouraged by rabbis concerned with preserving the Yiddish language and protecting congregants from the progressive influence of German culture. During the late 19th and early 20th century, a reverse trend toward emancipation and assimilation had developed among Jews in both Germany and Austria so that assimilated urbanized German Jews often thought of themselves more as Germans than Jews. Nevertheless, there was a malevolent anti-Semitism alive in central Europe. Clearly, the fate of six million Jews was not based on their inability to produce or to work but grew from a virulent hatred spawned hundreds of years earlier that came to full maturation under Hitler. Hitler boasted in 1908 that he was an anti-Semite. The tangible manifestation of Hitler's personal bigotry—the holocaust—came much later.

The Holocaust and Nazi Germany's cruel treatment of those considered to be undesirables cannot be used legitimately or honestly to support a simplistic argument linking slippery slope and euthanasia. Maltreatment of Jews preceded Hitler. Hitler's elimination-of-the-Jews policy was an overt expression of a current feeling that had festered for centuries in Europe and indeed is still present in parts of Europe and in the United States.

The slippery slope pattern cannot develop in America, so long as the government is of the people, for the people and by the people, and so long as the national ethic endorses the right to life, liberty and the pursuit of happiness for all citizens.

"I wish that the civil rights violation of legalizing assisted suicide based on health status were as obvious to everyone as it would be if assisted suicide were legalized based on gender or race."

LEGALIZING VOLUNTARY EUTHANASIA WOULD THREATEN THE DISABLED

Diane Coleman

In the following viewpoint, Diane Coleman maintains that voluntary euthanasia should not be legalized because it would violate the civil rights of disabled persons. According to Coleman, the majority of people whom Jack Kevorkian has helped commit suicide have been disabled, not terminally ill. She charges that Kevorkian's ability to avoid prosecution and to garner media attention for his activities reveals people's tendency to devalue the lives of the disabled. The author contends that if assisted suicide were legalized, it would mostly be offered to, or even forced upon, the disabled. Diane Coleman is president of the activist group Not Dead Yet.

As you read, consider the following questions:

1. What is the largest minority group in the country, according to Coleman?
2. What does Stephen Drake, as quoted by the author, say is Dr. Kevorkian's primary agenda?
3. What danger does the author fear people with spinal or head injuries may face in the critical period after injury?

Excerpted from Diane Coleman, "Disabled Activists Outraged by Kevorkian's Media Circus," a Not Dead Yet press release, November 23, 1998. Reprinted with permission from the author.

On November 22, 1998, on CBS's *60 Minutes*, an entire nation witnessed Jack Kevorkian's video-taped killing of a 52-year-old man with ALS [Lou Gehrig's Disease]. Since 1990, Kevorkian admits assisting in the suicides of over 120 individuals. According to the *Detroit Free Press*, the overwhelming majority of these individuals have been people who did not have terminal illnesses, but people who had disabilities, often less severe than my own.

NOT DEAD YET

My name is Diane Coleman and I am founder and President of Not Dead Yet, a national activist group leading the disabled community's fight against legalization of assisted suicide and euthanasia. If Kevorkian were assisting members of any other minority group to die, gays or African-Americans for example, he would be in jail by now and would never have gotten the bully pulpit of *60 Minutes* for the atrocity he committed. But *60 Minutes*, and most of the media, have long supported his cause as socially *progressive*, without ever even considering the views of the minority group to which his victims belong. The fact that he is still on the streets is not because our suicides are in fact fundamentally different, more justified than other people's suicides, but because society's prejudice against us is so deep and pervasive that we are seen as better off dead. A biased media has made Kevorkian a hero, so much so that juries of non-disabled people won't convict him—yet.

How many more of our people must die before he is brought to justice? According to the U.S. census, people with disabilities, seniors, adults and children, are the largest minority group in the country. We have the highest unemployment rate of all minorities; not because we can't work, but because employers and health insurance companies won't accept us. So people lose their jobs, can't get new jobs, and are forced into poverty. Families and friends often abandon people with disabilities, or treat them like unwanted burdens. It's hard to get the home health and support services that our health care system should provide to make things easier. Many people find themselves in human warehouses called nursing homes.

Most people don't know very much about the history of the disability rights movement. Our struggles have been fought on the margins of society's awareness. Few are aware of the hundreds of us who were arrested and jailed in the fight for passage of the Americans with Disabilities Act. We've rarely been on the media's radar screen, except as tragic but courageous human interest stories, objects of pity in Jerry Lewis' Telethon. The public doesn't know about the war we are now waging to free our brothers and sisters from nursing homes. As far as the network news is concerned, our political movement does not exist.

But suddenly the victims of our struggle have been thrown into the limelight, not the leaders of our civil rights marches, not our crusaders in Washington, not the countless unsung heroes who fight each day against poverty and human isolation, but the victims of Jack Kevorkian who gave up in their struggle and found a serial killer folk hero and his lawyer who built fame from the destruction of their lives. Perhaps for the first time, our movement is not on the margins, but at the center of a major public debate. . . .

ABLE-ISM

Some people say that assisted suicide is just a personal choice, exercising control over one's own body. *Choice* is nice rhetoric to borrow, but that's not what's really going on, is it? If it were just a matter of choice, our society would offer that choice to any competent adult. But no euthanasia group is suggesting that.

According to Stephen Drake, Not Dead Yet's leading expert on Kevorkian, *The press have ignored his primary agenda to push for a class of human beings on which doctors can do live experimentation and organ harvesting. In his book,* Prescription Medicide, *he writes that assisted suicide is just a first step to achieving public acceptance of this agenda.* In written testimony that Kevorkian submitted in his first trial, he said, *The voluntary self-elimination of individual and mortally diseased or crippled lives taken collectively can only enhance the preservation of public health and welfare. . . .*

Now people ask, *Are we worried about Kevorkian becoming a martyr if he starves himself in jail?* No. The real martyrs are his victims, martyrs to society's bigotry. It's called able-ism. And it's just as deadly as racism, just as wrong as sexism. If Kevorkian were a racist killer, he'd be in jail.

Some argue, *Yes, we have laws governing how society will normally respond to prevent suicide, but we can carve out an exception to those laws for certain people. After all, these people may need help to do it.*

Sometimes analogies are helpful. According to the *Detroit Free Press,* four out of five completed suicides are by men, but women try to commit suicide three times as often as men. Would we consider legalizing assisted suicide for women? This could be done with usual so-called safeguards, requiring that the woman make the request for assistance two times in a fourteen-day period, and is not being coerced in any way evident to two disinterested witnesses who have no financial stake in her demise. Don't we want to make sure that women can exercise their choice for suicide and not risk botching the attempt?

Well, I think anyone can see that a law like that would constitute illegal sex discrimination.

WHEN ASSISTED DEATH IS A READY SOLUTION

In fact, people with disabilities have already been endangered by relaxation of laws and policies protecting their lives. Medical rehabilitation specialists report that quadriplegics and other significantly disabled people are dying wrongfully in increasing numbers because emergency room physicians judge their quality of life as low and, therefore, withhold aggressive treatment. . . . Children with non-terminal disabilities who never asked to die are killed "gently" by the denial of routine treatment. People with relatively mild disabilities are routinely denied life saving organ transplants. . . .

In the Netherlands, where disabled children and adults with multiple sclerosis, quadriplegia, and depression are commonly assisted to die, disabled citizens express fear. Some carry wallet cards asking not to be euthanized. Dutch physicians follow a practice not to offer assisted ventilation to quadriplegics. Those who visit the U.S. have expressed surprise to see quadriplegics actively engaged in life with the use of costly portable ventilators and mouth-controlled power wheelchairs. Not surprisingly, the hospice movement is virtually non-existent in the Netherlands. When assisted death is a ready solution, there is little incentive to develop life-enhancing supportive services for "incurables."

Diane Coleman and Carol Gill, testimony before the U.S. House of Representatives, April 29, 1996.

I wish that the civil rights violation of legalizing assisted suicide based on health status were as obvious to everyone as it would be if assisted suicide were legalized based on gender or race. It is obvious to the following national disability organizations which have adopted positions opposing legalization of assisted suicide: the National Council on Independent Living, the National Council on Disability, the World Institute on Disability, American Disabled for Attendant Programs Today (ADAPT), Justice for All, TASH [the Association for Persons with Severe Handicaps], the National Spinal Cord Injury Association, the World Association of Persons With Disabilities and, of course, Not Dead Yet. Why are we ignored?

THE SUPPORT FOR EUTHANASIA

Why has the media been so biased in favor of the euthanasia movement? Why have they excluded the voices of the endangered minority from the euthanasia debate? Assisted suicide has been portrayed as a progressive social cause, ignoring its implications in a society with over 40 million uninsured.

Michigan voters, including a large majority of African-Americans, just defeated an assisted suicide referendum. Meanwhile in Oregon, where assisted suicide has been legalized, the Medicaid agency is cutting a variety of health services important to the disabled and chronically ill, and at the same time planning to fund assisted suicide.

Who are the lead proponents of assisted suicide? The Hemlock Society, whose members have a median income of $52,000 a year. They are the 4 W's, the white well-off worried well. And they don't care how many of our people are encouraged, even pressured, to die, so long as they themselves can have the security of a clean, neat, sanitized suicide at the hands of a medical professional. While Hemlock lobbyists continue to maintain a public perception that they are only talking about voluntary assisted suicide for terminally ill people, their proposed legislation in fact extends to all people with incurable conditions. See it on their web site. In addition, on December 3rd, 1997, the Hemlock Society issued a widely ignored press release which asked that family members and other *agents* be able to procure court orders to kill *a demented parent, a suffering severely disable (sic) spouse, or a child* if their lives are *too burdensome to continue.* That's involuntary euthanasia. . . .

A DUTY TO DIE?

Bioethicists are now writing about health care economics and the idea that some of us, whose health care services will cut into insurance company profits, have a duty to die, voluntarily or not. Especially in these days of managed care and government health care budget cuts, older and disabled people have a lot to be worried about. Society is struggling with policy issues that all come down to the question of whether people are more or less important than profits.

For the majority of people with disabilities, whose only information about living with disability comes from health care providers, today's trends do not bode well. I am especially concerned about newly injured people. Eight thousand new people are spinal cord injured each year, and 99,000 are hospitalized with moderate to severe head injuries. In critical periods after injury, people and their families could easily be swayed to make a so-called *choice* for death. So many of my colleagues with disabilities who now enjoy their lives have told me that they doubt they would have survived the first stages of their injuries in today's climate.

But do the media examine this larger social context in an objective way? Not so far. In fact, when Mike Wallace interviewed a disabled woman earlier in 1998, he asked her if she wanted to go to Kevorkian. She said she didn't want to die now, even though she did not think she wanted to be alive ten years from now. Then he asked her if she felt like a burden on society, and discussed the costs of her health care. Jimmy the Greek and Andy Rooney were disciplined for insulting gays and African-Americans, but Mike Wallace can get away with openly questioning the value of a disabled woman's life and making a hero out of a serial killer of our minority.

GETTING AWAY WITH MURDER

We disabled people begin to feel like we are in the South in the 1950's, where a killer could get away with murder based on the minority status of their victim. Kevorkian belongs in jail—it's the only way to stop him from killing one more disabled person. We demand that the Michigan prosecutor do his duty. Bring him to justice.

"The right to die movement will never have the intention to eliminate vulnerable populations, including the disabled."

LEGALIZING VOLUNTARY EUTHANASIA WOULD NOT THREATEN THE DISABLED

Hemlock Society

In the following viewpoint, the Hemlock Society, a national right-to-die organization, responds to the claim that legalizing voluntary euthanasia would put disabled persons at risk of being killed without their consent. The Hemlock Society maintains that it supports voluntary euthanasia only for mentally competent, terminally ill individuals who specifically and repeatedly request it. According to the authors, there is no evidence that disabled persons have anything to fear from the right-to-die movement. Unfounded fears, the Hemlock Society concludes, should not impede efforts to make assisted suicide legal for suffering, dying patients.

As you read, consider the following questions:

1. What percentage of Americans support the legalization of physician aid in dying, according to the Hemlock Society?
2. What evidence does the organization Not Dead Yet have for its claim that doctors are "too quick to assume that disabled people are 'better off dead,'" according to one author?
3. What claim made by disabled advocacy groups does the Hemlock Society call "an absurd logic"?

Reprinted, with permission, from the Hemlock Society's online letter "Hemlock Society Challenges Disabled on Opposition to Assisted Dying," at www.hemlock.org.

The Hemlock Society USA, a 19-year-old grass roots, right to die organization with more than 25,000 members in 80 chapters, takes issue with organizations representing the disabled in their opposition to the right of dying patients to seek help from their doctor in hastening their death. While recognizing the needs of the disabled community to achieve recognition and medical assistance, we support legislation which insures that a request for assistance in dying is *voluntary, enduring, monitored, and from a person who is already in the dying process.*

The Hemlock Society has many members who are disabled. Indeed, having a chronic, terminal illness generally renders a person disabled. People join Hemlock to support the idea that when death is inevitable they can retain their dignity in the face of irreversible suffering and degradation by making a choice not to prolong the dying process. This can be done legally, if they are on a respirator, or receiving other treatment which they can stop or refuse. If they are not being kept alive by treatment of some sort, then they have no legal option to hasten their death except to buy a gun, use a plastic bag, or implicate their friends or doctors in an illegal death. This does not imply that Hemlock regards people with disabilities as automatically wanting to die. It is up to each individual to determine for themselves when their quality of life is unendurable. We respect the right to want to *live* as much as the right to want to die.

Many Hemlock members also join disabled advocacy groups to promote a better life for disabled people—and indeed they have been quite successful in getting the Americans for Disabilities Act passed and generally making the plight of disabled people known to legislators. But many still want the right, as do able-bodied people, to choose a hastened death.

Where Is the Evidence?

The arguments of Not Dead Yet (NDY) and their parent organization American Disabled for Attendant Programs Today (ADAPT) take issue with progress in patients' rights and autonomy that have been made over the past 20 years. They claim that they are discriminated against in the medical system and are "being killed" by health care professionals who believe they are "better off dead." Where is the evidence? We have evidence on our side that doctors help people die illegally, that many people are so desperate that they make botched attempts, and that 75% of Americans do want to see such a law.

Even the staunchest opponents of physician aid in dying agree that a patient has the right to refuse treatment, including food and hydration and resuscitation. So many Americans have seen the prolonged, high tech, relentless attempts to prolong the dying process that they worry more about finding a doctor who will help them die than one who is good at keeping them alive!

If, as NDY claims, health care professionals are too quick to assume that disabled people are "better off dead"—a claim for which we have no evidence—then Hemlock will be the first to argue that this is an abuse of the current laws. If, as they claim, people with severe disability must sign "death warrants" or do not resuscitate (DNR) orders to obtain treatment we would certainly fight on their side to insure that this is not the case. But, we would not argue to rescind these hard-won rights but rather to correct the abuses. The entire thrust of the patients' rights movement has been to insure that health care professionals listen to and follow *what the patient wants*. This is the point of advance directives, patient control over DNR orders, the Patient Self-Determination Act, and all proposed laws about physician aid in dying.

THE SIMPLE TRUTH

The simple truth is that physician-assisted death for the terminally ill has nothing to do with the disabled. Disabled people are not terminally ill. Aid in dying would be available only upon repeated request and only to terminally ill individuals for whom death is imminent. I have encountered the convoluted assertion that to say aid in dying has nothing to do with disabled people is to deny that terminally ill people are disabled. But this is an irrelevant statement devoid of any logical significance. The relevant fact is that the vast majority of disabled people are not terminally ill. A person must be terminally ill to request physician aid in dying, period.

Barbara Dority, Humanist, July/August 1997.

To legalize aid in dying will bring it out of the darkness in which it now exists on a widespread basis to a situation in which the patient's request is witnessed, in writing, the diagnosis is confirmed by a second opinion, and penalties are in force to guard against coercion.

The claim that everyone is "cheaper dead than alive" may be a general indictment of our managed care system. Every effort must be made by organized medicine in this country to insure that all Americans get adequate health care without incentives to not treat. But while we are protecting that flank—and improving care for the terminally ill—let us not forget that a gentle, certain, painless assisted death is an option that should not be denied to the dying while they wait for all systems to be perfected.

AN ABSURD LOGIC

NDY and ADAPT argue that people with severe disabilities are denied equal protection of the law since assisted suicide would only apply to people with illnesses and disabilities. If the courts were to recognize a right to assisted suicide, they argue, the provisions should apply universally regardless of health or disability status. This is an absurd logic. We are talking about the ability of people who are already dying to ask for help in hastening death—not everyone who is suicidal. If it were the case that assistance in dying were universally available the disabled and the able-bodied would indeed be in jeopardy.

Disabled persons have every right to protect their interests—but *not* at the expense of the rest of us. The majority of Americans agree with the legalization of physician aid in dying for mentally competent, terminally ill people who request it. This has been Hemlock's mission for 17 years. No proposed legislation has included people with mental or physical disabilities *except* if he or she were terminally ill and because of their suffering chose to *ask* for help to die. The right to die movement will never have the intention to eliminate vulnerable populations, including the disabled. Hemlock has made it clear that this must be a *voluntary, personal* choice in the context of *safeguards* against abuse.

| "It is not possible to sanction and regulate euthanasia within any prescribed guidelines."

SAFEGUARDS CANNOT PREVENT ABUSE OF LEGALIZED EUTHANASIA

Herbert Hendin

Herbert Hendin argues in the following viewpoint that, in practice, it is impossible to regulate legalized euthanasia so that it is limited to terminally ill, mentally competent patients who request it. Hendin contends that legalized euthanasia in the Netherlands has encouraged doctors there to accept euthanasia as a routine practice, and that in many instances doctors have ended the lives of patients without their request. He believes the Dutch experience clearly illustrates that even extensive legal safeguards cannot prevent euthanasia from being abused once it is initially permitted. Hendin is executive director of the American Suicide Foundation and author of the book *Seduced by Death: Doctors, Patients, and the Dutch Cure.*

As you read, consider the following questions:

1. What is the name of the report commissioned by the Dutch government to study the problem of "involuntary euthanasia"?
2. What portion of Dutch doctors feel it is appropriate to introduce the subject of euthanasia to their patients, according to Hendin?
3. In the author's view, why is supervisory review of suspicious euthanasia cases after the euthanasia has been performed ineffective?

Excerpted from Herbert Hendin's testimony before the U.S. House of Representatives Committee on the Judiciary, Subcommittee on the Constitution, April 29, 1996.

In the spring of 1993 a Dutch court in Assen ruled that a psychiatrist was justified in assisting in the suicide of his patient, a physically healthy but grief-stricken 50-year-old social worker who was mourning the death of her son and who came to the psychiatrist saying she wanted death, not treatment. I had a chance to spend about seven hours interviewing the psychiatrist involved. Without going into the details of the case . . . it is worth noting that the psychiatrist assisted in the patient's suicide a little over two months after she came to see him, about four months after her younger son died of cancer at 20. Discussion of the case centered around whether the psychiatrist, supported by experts, was right in his contention that the woman suffered from an understandable and untreatable grief. Although no one should underestimate the grief of a mother who has lost a beloved child, life offers ways to cope with such grief and time alone was likely to have altered her mood.

The Dutch Supreme Court which ruled on the Assen Case in June 1994 agreed with the lower courts in affirming that mental suffering can be grounds for euthanasia, but felt that in the absence of physical illness a psychiatric consultant should have actually seen the patient. Since it felt that in all other regards the psychiatrist had behaved responsibly it imposed no punishment. Since the consultation can easily be obtained from a sympathetic colleague, it offers the patient little protection. The case was seen as a triumph by euthanasia advocates since it legally established mental suffering as a basis for euthanasia.

FROM ASSISTED SUICIDE TO INVOLUNTARY EUTHANASIA

Over the past two decades, the Netherlands has moved from assisted suicide to euthanasia, from euthanasia for the terminally ill to euthanasia for the chronically ill, from euthanasia for physical illness to euthanasia for psychological distress and from voluntary euthanasia to nonvoluntary and involuntary euthanasia.

Once the Dutch accepted assisted suicide it was not possible legally or morally to deny more active medical help; i.e., euthanasia to those who could not effect their own deaths. Nor could they deny assisted suicide or euthanasia to the chronically ill who have longer to suffer than the terminally ill or to those who have psychological pain not associated with physical disease. To do so would be a form of discrimination. Involuntary euthanasia has been justified as necessitated by the need to make decisions for patients not competent to choose for themselves.

That it is often the doctor and not the patient who determines the choice for death was underlined by the documentation of "involuntary euthanasia" in the Remmelink report—the Dutch government's commissioned study of the problem. "Involuntary euthanasia" is a term that is disturbing to the Dutch. The Dutch define euthanasia as the ending of the life of one person by another at the first person's request. If life is ended without request they do not consider it to be euthanasia. The Remmelink report uses the equally troubling expression "termination of the patient without explicit request" to refer to euthanasia performed without consent on competent, partially competent, and incompetent patients.

The report revealed that in over 1,000 cases, of the 130,000 deaths in the Netherlands each year, physicians admitted they actively caused or hastened death without any request from the patient. In about 25,000 cases, medical decisions were made at the end of life that might or were intended to end the life of the patient without consulting the patient. In nearly 20,000 of these cases (about 80 percent) physicians gave the patient's impaired ability to communicate as their justification for not seeking consent.

This left about 5,000 cases in which physicians made decisions that might or were intended to end the lives of competent patients without consulting them. In 13 percent of these cases, physicians who did not communicate with competent patients concerning decisions that might or were intended to end their lives gave as a reason for not doing so that they had previously had some discussion of the subject with the patient. Yet it seems incomprehensible that a physician would terminate the life of a competent patient on the basis of some prior discussion without checking if the patient still felt the same way.

PATIENTS DO NOT HAVE CONTROL

A number of Dutch euthanasia advocates have admitted that practicing euthanasia with legal sanction has encouraged doctors to feel that they can make life or death decisions without consulting patients. Many advocates privately defend the need for doctors to end the lives of competent patients without discussion with them. An attorney who represents the Dutch Voluntary Euthanasia Society gave me as an example a case in which a doctor had terminated the life of a nun a few days before she would have died because she was in excruciating pain but her religious convictions did not permit her to ask for death. He did not argue when I asked why she should not have been permitted to die in the way she wanted.

Even when the patient requests or consents to euthanasia, in cases presented to me in the Netherlands and cases I have reviewed in this country, assisted suicide and euthanasia were usually the result of an interaction in which the needs and character of family, friends, and doctor play as big and often bigger role than those of the patient.

FALSE ASSURANCES

U.S. euthanasia advocates blithely assure us that this country will learn from the Dutch mistakes so that such abuses never happen here. There's only one problem with that assurance: Violations of euthanasia-type guidelines have already happened here.

In 1986 and again in 1992, the American Medical Association's Council on Ethical and Judicial Affairs issued ethical opinions designed to define the circumstances under which terminally ill and permanently unconscious patients could ethically be starved and dehydrated. These guidelines permitted "technologically supplied" food and fluids to be withdrawn from terminally ill people "whose death is imminent" and from unconscious patients whose coma or persistent vegetative state is "beyond doubt irreversible."

Despite these easily understood restrictions, people who were not terminally ill nor unconscious have also had their "medical treatment" of food and fluids withheld. This expanded practice has even received the approval of some courts. The A.M.A. then expanded the guidelines to comport with actual clinical practice. . . .

Protective guidelines give the appearance of normalcy and protection while offering no actual shelter from abuse. Worse, they act subversively to hide the truth about the victims of euthanasia. In short, guidelines serve no useful purpose other than to provide false assurances to the public.

Wesley J. Smith, *Forced Exit: The Slippery Slope from Assisted Suicide to Legalized Murder*, 1997.

In a study of euthanasia done in Dutch hospitals, doctors and nurses reported that more requests for euthanasia came from families than from patients themselves. The investigator concluded that the families, the doctors, and the nurses were involved in pressuring patients to request euthanasia.

A Dutch medical journal noted an example of a wife who no longer wished to care for her sick husband; she gave him a choice between euthanasia and admission to a home for the chronically ill. The man, afraid of being left to the mercy of strangers in an unfamiliar place, chose to be killed. The doctor, although aware of the coercion, ended the man's life.

EUTHANASIA HAS BECOME ROUTINE

The Remmelink report revealed that more than half of Dutch physicians considered it appropriate to introduce the subject of euthanasia to their patients. Virtually all the medical advocates of euthanasia that I spoke to in the Netherlands saw this as enabling the patient to consider an option that he or she may have felt inhibited about bringing up, rather than a form of coercion. They seemed not to recognize that the doctor was also telling the patient that his or her life was not worth living, a message that would have a powerful effect on the patient's outlook and decision.

The Dutch experience illustrates how social sanction promotes a culture that transforms suicide into assisted suicide and euthanasia and encourages patients and doctors to see assisted suicide and euthanasia—intended as an unfortunate necessity in exceptional cases—as almost a routine way of dealing with serious or terminal illness.

Pressure for improved palliative care appears to have evaporated in the Netherlands. Discussion of care for the terminally ill is dominated by how and when to extend assisted suicide and euthanasia to increasing groups of patients. Given the inequities in our own health care system and the inadequacies of our care of those who are terminally ill, palliative care would be an even more likely casualty of euthanasia in this country. Euthanasia will become a way for all of us to ignore the genuine needs of terminally ill people.

The public has the illusion that legalizing assisted suicide and euthanasia will give them greater autonomy. If the Dutch experience teaches us anything it is that the reverse is true. In practice it is still the doctor who decides whether to perform euthanasia. He can suggest it, not give patients obvious alternatives, ignore patients' ambivalence, and even put to death patients who have not requested it. Euthanasia enhances the power and control of doctors, not patients.

People assume that the doctor encouraging or supporting assisted suicide is making as objective a judgment as a radiologist reading an x-ray. The decisive role of the physician's needs and values in the decision for euthanasia are not apparent to them.

GUIDELINES ARE IGNORED

Virtually every guideline set up by the Dutch to regulate euthanasia has been modified or violated with impunity. Despite their best efforts, the Dutch have been able to get only 60 percent of their doctors to report their euthanasia cases (and there is reason from the Remmelink report to question whether all of them are reporting truthfully). Since following the legal guidelines would free from the risk of prosecution the 40 percent of Dutch doctors who admit to not reporting their cases and the 20 percent who say that under no circumstances will they do so, it is a reasonable assumption that these doctors are not following the guidelines. The cases presented to me and to Dr. Carlos Gomez bear this out. Dr. Gomez and I went to the Netherlands at different times and with totally different perspectives, since he is a palliative care specialist and I am a psychiatrist. Yet after hearing detailed cases of euthanasia presented by Dutch physicians, we independently came to the same conclusion: that it is not possible to sanction and regulate euthanasia within any prescribed guidelines.

A supervisory system intended to protect patients would require an ombudsman to look at the overall situation including the family, the patient, the doctor, and, above all, the interaction among them prior to the performance of assisted suicide or euthanasia. This would involve an intrusion into the relationship between patient and doctor that most patients would not want and most doctors would not accept.

Without such intrusion before the fact, there is no law or set of guidelines that can protect patients. After euthanasia has been performed, since only the patient and the doctor may know the actual facts of the case, and since only the doctor is alive to relate them, any medical, legal, or interdisciplinary review committee will, as in the Netherlands, only know what the doctor chooses to tell them. Legal sanction creates a permissive atmosphere that seems to foster not taking the guidelines too seriously. The notion that those American doctors—who are admittedly breaking some serious laws in now assisting in a suicide— would follow guidelines if assisted suicide were legalized is not borne out by the Dutch experience; nor is it likely given the failure of American practitioners of assisted suicide to follow elementary safeguards in cases they have published.

ASSISTED SUICIDE WOULD REPLACE PALLIATIVE CARE

Patients who request euthanasia are usually asking in the strongest way they know for mental and physical relief from suffering. When that request is made to a caring, sensitive, and knowledgeable physician who can address their fear, relieve their suffering, and assure them that he or she will remain with them to the end, most patients no longer want to die and are grateful for the time remaining to them.

Advances in our knowledge of palliative care in the past twenty years make clear that humane care for the terminally ill does not require us to legalize assisted suicide and euthanasia. Study has shown that the more physicians know about palliative care the less apt they are to favor legalizing assisted suicide and euthanasia. Our challenge is to bring that knowledge and that care to all patients who are terminally ill.

Our success in meeting the challenge of providing palliative care for those who are terminally ill will do much to preserve our social humanity. If we do not provide such care, legalization of assisted suicide and euthanasia will become the simplistic answer to the problems of dying. If legalization prevails, we will lose more lives to suicide (although we will call the deaths by a different name) than can be saved by the efforts of the American Suicide Foundation and those of all the other institutions working to prevent suicide in this country.

The tragedy that will befall depressed suicidal patients will be matched by what will happen to terminally ill people, particularly older poor people. Assisted suicide and euthanasia will become routine ways of dealing with serious and terminal illness just as they have in the Netherlands; those without means will be under particular pressure to accept the euthanasia option. In the process, palliative care will be undercut for everyone.

Euthanasia advocates have come to see suicide as a cure for disease and a way of appropriating death's power over the human capacity for control. They have detoured what could be a constructive effort to manage the final phase of life in more varied and individualistic ways. Our social policy must be based on a larger and more positive concern for people who are terminally ill. It must reflect an expansive determination to relieve their physical pain, to discover the nature of their fears, and to diminish suffering by providing meaningful reassurance of the life that has been lived and is still going on.

"While most of the concerns [about legalizing physician-assisted suicide] do not hold up under scrutiny, some are valid and must be addressed through stringent safeguards."

SAFEGUARDS CAN PREVENT ABUSE OF LEGALIZED EUTHANASIA

Part I: David Orentlicher, Part II: Robert Young

In the first part of the following two-part viewpoint, David Orentlicher contends that the potential for doctors to abuse physician-assisted suicide can be reduced by requiring patients who choose suicide to self-administer the fatal dose of medication. Orentlicher is a professor of law and former director of the American Medical Association's Division of Medical Ethics. In the second part, Robert Young, a professor of philosophy at La Trobe University in Victoria, Australia, argues that the Dutch policy of permitting voluntary euthanasia has not been widely abused, as many critics have charged.

As you read, consider the following questions:

1. In Orentlicher's view, what types of specialists should consult with the patient before a request for physician-assisted suicide is granted?
2. In Young's opinion, what does the Dutch public's support for their nation's euthanasia policies suggest?

Part I: Reprinted from David Orentlicher, "Navigating the Narrows of Doctor-Assisted Suicide," *Technology Review*, July 1996, vol. 99, published by the Association of Alumni and Alumnae of MIT, copyright 1996. Reproduced by permission of the publisher via Copyright Clearance Center, Inc. Part II: Excerpted from Robert Young, "Euthanasia, Voluntary," 1996, *Stanford Encyclopedia of Philosophy*, http://plato.stanford.edu/archives/win1998/entries/euthanasia-voluntary/, with permission from the author. (Bibliographical references in the original have been omitted from this reprint.)

I

After years of debate, prompted by high-profile cases such as those involving Jack Kevorkian, our laws may soon widely recognize a right to physician-assisted suicide. Two federal appeals courts, with jurisdictions including New York, California, and nine other states, have held that terminally ill patients have a constitutional right to this way of ending life. And in Oregon, a public referendum has resulted in the enactment of a statutory right to assisted suicide for terminally ill residents.

Opponents of assisted suicide—including the American Medical Association—have argued that its legalization poses serious threats to the welfare of patients and the ethics of the medical profession. While most of the concerns do not hold up under scrutiny, some are valid and must be addressed through stringent safeguards.

Many commentators say there is no need for assisted suicide as long as doctors provide adequate pain control. These observers point out that more needs to be done to ensure that dying patients receive enough medication for their pain. Still, some patients' pain cannot be alleviated even with the most aggressive treatment. More important, physical pain is not the only cause of intolerable suffering. Many dying patients want to end their lives because of their utter dependence on others, the wasting of the body into little more than flesh and bones, the loss of control over bodily functions, the unrelieved mental and physical exhaustion, and the knowledge that things will only grow worse.

People who oppose doctor-assisted suicide have also pointed out the real risk that the practice may extend to inappropriate cases. Vulnerable patients could ask to end their lives because of pressures from family, caregivers, or insurers, and they may be influenced by arguments about the burden that treatment for dying patients places on society's limited resources. Patients seeking assisted suicide may be suffering from treatable depression or the side effects of medication, and doctors might not always be adequately trained to distinguish requests that are rational from those that are not. Moreover, physicians sometimes find that caring for patients who are seriously ill is time-consuming and psychologically draining, and may thus respond to entreaties for assisted suicide too readily.

SAFEGUARDS RATHER THAN A PROHIBITION

Society should address these possibilities with safeguards rather than a prohibition, just as has been done when requests for withdrawal of life-sustaining treatment have posed similar risks.

A specialist in pain relief and other palliative measures should ensure that all appropriate care has been provided to patients asking for the means to hasten the dying process. To ensure that a request for assisted suicide is truly voluntary and not the result of moral incapacity or undue pressure, a psychiatric specialist should fully evaluate the requesting patient. And a social-services specialist should determine that all other support services have been considered, such as home hospice care, which some patients might prefer over assisted suicide.

ACTIVE EUTHANASIA IN THE NETHERLANDS, 1990–1995		
	1990	1995
Total number of deaths in the country	128,786	135,675
Requests for euthanasia/assistance in suicide	9,000	9,700
Active euthanasia upon request of the patient	2,300	3,200
Assisted suicides	400	400
Active euthanasia without explicit request of the patient	1,000	900
Intentional lethal overdose of morphine-like drugs:		
with consent of the patient	3,159	2,046
without the patient's knowledge	4,941	1,889

Paul J. van der Maas et al., *Euthanasia and Other Medical Decisions Concerning the End of Life,* 1992, and Gerrit van der Wal and Paul J. van der Maas, *Euthanasia and Other Medical Decisions Concerning the End of Life,* 1996.

Still, critics point out that some doctors might want to disregard such safeguards. Multiple consultations take time and cost money, and physicians may be tempted to shortcut the process. The risks of abuse are real, according to findings from the Netherlands, where doctor-assisted suicide and euthanasia are practiced. In 1991 researchers reported that Dutch physicians had not fulfilled the country's procedural requirements in more than 25 percent of the cases involving these methods of dying. But the United States can avoid a similar experience. Since in Holland the primary abuse has been the administration of euthanasia by doctors without the patient's clear consent, U.S. laws can continue to prohibit euthanasia and insist that the right to assisted suicide be limited to patients who can self-administer the fatal dose of medication. While this requirement would deny death to patients so incapacitated they cannot take drugs by themselves, the right to assisted suicide should not be extended too far.

Moreover, laws should permit doctors to assist in the suicide only of terminally ill patients. Such a limitation would not only restrict the procedure to a justified group but would also tie the practice to the reason society has strongly supported a right to refuse life-sustaining treatment. For example, in its 1976 landmark opinion in the case of Karen Quinlan, the New Jersey Supreme Court observed that treatment withdrawal should be permitted when the patient's prognosis becomes very poor and the degree of bodily invasion from treatment becomes very high. To ensure that a person has reached such a stage, a second, independent physician with expertise in the patient's illness should confirm any diagnosis and prognosis.

To a certain extent, the courts can implement safeguards for assisted suicide. But years may be needed for cases to work themselves through all levels of appeals, and court decisions often address only part of an issue at a time. Legislatures can move more quickly, and should address the topic of assisted suicide comprehensively after analyzing the full range of perspectives. State legislatures should handle this issue because experimentation by different states will help sort out the best approaches, a process the courts have long held important.

THE LIFE-PROLONGING EFFECT OF PATIENT CONTROL

As legislatures and the courts develop and insist on safeguards, they would do well to recognize that permitting doctor-assisted suicide will actually prolong some patients' lives. What patients often want is not so much the ability to die but the knowledge that they have control over the timing of their death. Once such control is permitted, they may be more willing to undergo aggressive medical treatments that are painful and risky. If a treatment does not succeed but only worsens the patient's condition, the person is assured that he or she can end the suffering.

We have already seen the life-prolonging effects of patient control. Both Elizabeth Bouvia, who depended on a feeding tube, and Lawrence McAfee, who required a ventilator, sued to have their treatment stopped. But neither exercised that right once the courts recognized it. The two were willing to continue their lives upon receiving clear authority that they could decide whether and when their treatment would end.

By adopting stringent safeguards for doctor-assisted suicide, society can give dying patients the fundamental ability to decide how they wish to handle their suffering. And it can provide the critical assurance that they are protected from abuse.

II

It is often said that if society allows *voluntary* euthanasia to be legally permitted we will have set foot on a slippery slope that will lead us inevitably to support other forms of euthanasia, especially non-voluntary euthanasia. Whereas it was once the common refrain that that was precisely what happened in Hitler's Germany, nowadays the claim tends to be that the experience of the Netherlands in the last decade or so confirms the reality of the slippery slope. Slippery slope arguments come in at least three different versions: logical, psychological and arbitrary line. What the different forms share is the contention that once the first step is taken on a slippery slope the subsequent steps follow inexorably, whether for logical reasons, psychological reasons or to avoid arbitrariness in 'drawing a line' across a person's actions.

I shall first say something about why at the theoretical level none of these forms of argument appears powerful enough to trouble an advocate of the legalisation of voluntary euthanasia. I shall then, second, comment on the alleged empirical support from the experiences of Hitler's Germany and present day Holland for the existence of a slippery slope beginning from voluntary euthanasia.

THE SLIDE FROM VOLUNTARY TO
NON-VOLUNTARY EUTHANASIA IS NOT INEVITABLE

There is nothing logically inconsistent in supporting voluntary euthanasia but rejecting non-voluntary euthanasia as morally inappropriate. Since the two issues are logically separate there will be some advocates of voluntary euthanasia who will wish also to lend their support to some acts of non-voluntary euthanasia (e.g. for those in persistent vegetative states who have never indicated their wishes about being helped to die or for some severely disabled infants for whom the outlook is hopeless). Others will think that what may be done with the consent of the patient sets a strict limit on the practice of euthanasia. The difference is not one of logical acumen. It has to be located in the respective values of the different supporters (e.g. whether self-determination alone or the best interests of a person should prevail).

As regards the alleged psychological inevitability of moving from voluntary to non-voluntary euthanasia, again it is hard to see the supposed inevitability. Why should those who value the autonomy of the individual and so support provision for voluntary euthanasia be psychologically driven to support cases of euthanasia which have no connection with the exercise of patient autonomy?

Finally, if there is nothing arbitrary about distinguishing voluntary euthanasia from non-voluntary euthanasia (because the line between them is based on clear principles) there can be no substance to the charge that there is a slide from voluntary to non-voluntary euthanasia that can only be prevented by arbitrarily drawing a line between them.

What, though, of Hitler's Germany and today's Holland? The former is easily dismissed as a provider of evidence for an inevitable descent from voluntary euthanasia to non-voluntary. There never was a policy in favour of, or a legal practice of, voluntary euthanasia in Germany in the 1920s to the 1940s. There was, prior to Hitler coming to power, a clear practice of killing some disabled persons. The justification was never suggested to be that their being killed was in their best interests, rather it was said to be society that benefited. Hitler's later revival of the practice and its widening to take in other groups such as Jews and gypsies was part of a programme of *eugenics*, not euthanasia.

No Evidence of a Slippery Slope in the Netherlands

Since the publication of the Remmelink Report in 1991 into the medical practice of euthanasia in the Netherlands it has frequently been said that the Dutch experience shows decisively that legally protecting voluntary euthanasia is impossible without also affording protection to the non-voluntary euthanasia that will come in its train. Unfortunately, many of those who have made this claim have paid insufficient attention to the serious studies carried out by van der Maas, et al., and van der Wal, et al. into what the Report revealed. In a second nation-wide investigation of physician-assisted dying in the Netherlands carried out in 1995 a similar picture emerged as had in the earlier Remmelink Report. Again no evidence was found of any descent down a slippery slope toward ignoring people's voluntary choices to be assisted to die. The true picture is that, of those terminally ill persons assisted to die under the agreement between the legal and medical authorities, a little over one half were clearly cases of voluntary euthanasia as it has been characterised in this article. Of the remainder, the vast majority of cases were of patients who at the time of the assisted death were no longer competent. The deaths of some of these were brought about by withdrawal of treatment, that of others by interventions such as the giving of lethal doses of anaesthetics. But the critical point about this vast majority of such cases is that the decision to end life was nearly always taken after consultation between the doctor(s) and family members. In a very few cases there was no consultation of this kind. It seems that sometimes, at least, this was because families in the Netherlands strictly have no final authority to act as surrogate decision-makers for incompetent persons. That there has only been one prosecution of a Dutch doctor for failing to follow agreed procedures, and that the Dutch public have regularly reaffirmed their support for those agreed procedures suggests that, contrary to the claims of some critics of the Netherlands' experience of legally protecting voluntary euthanasia, social life has not broken down. Indeed, such studies as have been published about what happens in other countries, like Australia, where no legal protection is in place, suggest that the pattern of things in Holland and elsewhere is quite similar. If active euthanasia is widely practised but in ways that are not legally recognized there is apt in fact to be more danger that the distinction between voluntary cases and non-voluntary ones will be blurred or ignored than in a situation where the carrying out of euthanasia is transparent and subject to monitoring.

SAFEGUARDS CAN BE EFFECTIVE

We can bring this discussion of [slippery slope arguments] to a close with two observations. First, nothing that has been said should be taken as suggesting that there is no need to put in place safeguards against potential abuse of any legal protection for voluntary euthanasia. This is particularly important for those who have become incompetent by the time decisions need to be taken about assisting them to die. . . . There are ways of addressing this issue (such as by way of advance declarations or living wills) which are widely thought to be effective, even if they are not perfect. The main point to be stressed at the present, though, is that there is surely no need for anyone to be frightened into thinking that the legalisation of voluntary euthanasia will inevitably end in her having her life snatched away from her should she become incapable of exercising a competent judgement on her own behalf. Second, it is, of course, possible that the reform of any law may have unintended effects. It is sometimes said in discussions about legalising voluntary euthanasia that experience with abortion law reform should remind us of how quickly and easily practices can become accepted which were never among the reformers' intentions, and that the same thing could occur if voluntary euthanasia were to become legally permitted. No amount of theorising, it is said, can gainsay that possibility. There is no need to deny that it is possible that reform of the laws that presently prohibit voluntary euthanasia could have untoward consequences. However, if the arguments given above are sound (and the Dutch experience is not only the best evidence we have that they are sound, but the only relevant evidence), that does not seem very likely.

PERIODICAL BIBLIOGRAPHY

The following articles have been selected to supplement the diverse views presented in this chapter. Addresses are provided for periodicals not indexed in the *Readers' Guide to Periodical Literature*, the *Alternative Press Index*, the *Social Sciences Index*, or the *Index to Legal Periodicals and Books*.

Barbara Dority   "The Ultimate Civil Liberty," *Humanist*, July/August 1997.

Brian Eads   "A License to Kill," *Reader's Digest*, September 1997.

Ezekiel J. Emanuel and Margaret P. Battin   "What Are the Potential Cost Savings from Legalizing Physician-Assisted Suicide?" *New England Journal of Medicine*, July 16, 1998. Available from 10 Shattuck St., Boston, MA 02115-6094 or http://www.nejm.org.

Dinyar Godrej   "A Careful Death," *New Internationalist*, April 1997.

William Norman Grigg   "Abortion and Beyond," *New American*, January 19, 1998. Available from 770 Westhill Blvd., Appleton, WI 54914.

Steve Hallock   "Physician-Assisted Suicide: 'Slippery Slope' or Civil Right?" *Humanist*, July/August 1996.

Herbert Hendin   "Physician-Assisted Suicide: A Look at the Netherlands," *Current*, December 1997. Available from 1319 18th St. NW, Washington, DC 20036-1802.

Paul J. van der Maas et al.   "Euthanasia, Physician-Assisted Suicide, and Other Medical Practices Involving the End of Life in the Netherlands, 1990–1995," *New England Journal of Medicine*, November 28, 1996.

Diane E. Meier   "A Change of Heart on Assisted Suicide," *New York Times*, April 24, 1998.

Franklin G. Miller et al.   "Can Physician-Assisted Suicide Be Regulated Effectively?" *Journal of Law, Medicine & Ethics*, Fall 1996.

Wesley J. Smith   "Death March," *National Review*, February 23, 1998.

Ann G. Thunder   "Assisted Suicide: Managed Care," *Vital Speeches of the Day*, May 15, 1997.

CHAPTER 4

SHOULD PHYSICIANS ASSIST IN SUICIDE?

CHAPTER PREFACE

The euthanasia debate raises serious questions for dying patients and their families, as well as for ethicists and lawmakers. But many of the right-to-die movement's leaders, and many of its most outspoken opponents, are physicians.

"What is really at stake here is physician-assisted suicide," state authors Leon Kass and Nelson Lund, who are opposed to the practice. As Hemlock Society executive director Faye Girsh explains, "It is necessary for physicians to be the agents of death if the person wants to die quickly, safely, peacefully and non-violently, since the best means to accomplish this is medication that only doctors can prescribe."

Yet even ardent supporters of physician-assisted suicide are aware that many doctors object to the practice. Gerald Larue, in his book *Playing God: Fifty Religions' Views on Your Right to Die*, argues that dying patients should have access to physician-assisted euthanasia. But he also recognizes that "Some physicians . . . would not be willing to participate in an act of physician-assisted euthanasia. The right to make such choices without being condemned for their decision is theirs as free citizens and persons committed to a particular ethical position."

Larue believes that doctors who oppose assisted suicide should not be forced to act against their beliefs, but instead should refer patients who request aid in dying to a more willing doctor. "It would be incumbent on physicians to make clear to their patients their standing on this important issue," writes Larue. His position is echoed in Oregon's Measure 16, the voter initiative permitting physician-assisted suicide in that state. The law specifically states that physicians may refuse to participate in a suicide, and most proposals to legalize assisted suicide in other states have similar opt-out clauses.

The authors in the following chapter discuss physician-assisted suicide in the context of medical ethics. These medical perspectives on the euthanasia debate are especially important because even if some states choose to permit physician assistance in suicide, and terminally ill patients request it, it will still fall to individual doctors to choose, based on their own beliefs about morality and their duties as physicians, whether to grant such requests.

| "In some extreme, hopeless circumstances, the best service a physician can render may be to help a person hasten death."

ASSISTED SUICIDE IS AN ETHICALLY ACCEPTABLE PRACTICE FOR PHYSICIANS

Kenneth Cauthen

In the following viewpoint, Kenneth Cauthen argues that the duty of physicians is to do what is best for their patients, even if that means granting a request for physician-assisted suicide. Cauthen contends that in cases of extreme suffering, and when the patient requests it, assisted suicide is an act of compassion and benevolence. Kenneth Cauthen is a retired professor of theology and a Baptist minister as well as the author of several books, including *The Ethics of Assisted Death: When Life Becomes a Burden Too Hard to Bear*, from which the following viewpoint is adapted.

As you read, consider the following questions:

1. What question does Cauthen believe physicians should ask themselves regarding their duty to their patients?
2. In the author's view, where does the most powerful argument in favor of physician-assisted suicide come from?
3. How do many physicians help their patients to die, according to Cauthen?

Excerpted from Kenneth Cauthen, *The Ethics of Assisted Death: When Life Becomes a Burden Too Hard to Bear*, online version at www.frontiernet.net/~kenc/asuici.htm. Copyright ©1999. Reprinted by permission of CSS Publishing Company, PO Box 4503, Lima, Ohio 45802-4503.

Deciding what is right is especially difficult when the permissibility of deliberately ending a human life is involved. In these extreme situations the normal rules of morality are stretched to the breaking point. Self-defense against a would-be murderer, killing enemy soldiers in war, capital punishment for the most horrendous crimes, intentional suicide by a spy to prevent torture or a coerced disclosure of vital military information, killing a berserk man who is systematically murdering a line of hostages—all these instances pose questions that severely test our moral wisdom.

Nearly everyone would agree that in some of the cases listed it would be legitimate to end a life deliberately. This fact tells us that killing a person is not always and necessarily regarded as wrong. It all depends upon the circumstances. Now enters the question of physician-assisted death.

I want to make a cautious argument that under some carefully limited circumstances, it is permissible for a physician to assist a person hasten death to end unwanted, intolerable, unnecessary suffering. This includes providing medicines or other means the patient can use to commit suicide or by directly administering medicines that end the patient's life.

THE RIGHTS OF PATIENTS AND THE ROLE OF DOCTORS

1. *In some situations the choice of the patient takes priority over other considerations.* Consider a person with an incurable illness or severe debility such that life has become so racked with pain or so burdensome that desirable, meaningful, purposeful existence has ceased. Suppose that person says, "My life is no longer worth living; I cannot stand it any longer; I want to end it now to avoid further pain, indignity, torment, and despair." In the end after all alternatives have been thoroughly considered, I believe this person has the right to make a choice to die and that it ought to be honored. We would want to urge consultation with physicians, clergy, lawyers, therapists, family, and others so that such a serious and irreversible decision can be made after sufficient time has passed and every alternative thoroughly weighed. We have obligations to others and should take their needs into account. The state has an interest in protecting life. But, in the end, individuals should be given wide latitude in deciding when life has become an unendurable hardship.

2. *The role of the physician is to do what is best for the patient, and in some extreme situations this may include hastening death upon the voluntary request of the dying.* Many doctors protest that they are committed to preserve and enhance life, not to end it deliberately. If the role of

the physician is defined solely in terms of healing, then, of course, this excludes assisting someone to die. This is the wrong way to go about defining the scope and limits of the doctor's proper function. I suggest that the question should be put this way: What is the best thing I can do to help my patients in whatever circumstances arise, given my special knowledge and skills? In nearly every case the answer will be to heal, to prolong life, to reduce suffering, to restore health and physical well-being, i.e., to preserve and enhance life. But in some extreme, hopeless circumstances, the best service a physician can render may be to help a person hasten death in order to relieve intolerable, unnecessary suffering that makes life unbearable as judged by the patient. This would be an enlargement of the physician's role, not a contradiction of it.

MERCY KILLING

3. *Sometimes ending suffering takes priority over extending life.* Assisted death is so troubling because it involves an agonizing conflict between values. Life is a wonderful gift full of the promise of pleasure, joy, happiness, and love. But circumstances may turn it into a heartbreaking, hopeless burden filled with suffering, pain, and despair. We desire to live, but in some situations death may be preferable to the continuation of an intolerably burdensome existence. If some person comes to that dreadful conclusion, what is our duty? The moral imperative forbids us to kill, but it also enjoins us to be merciful. We have a term that puts the dilemma before us—mercy killing. While insisting that we must make every effort possible to guard against abuse, I sorrowfully conclude that, at a patient's request, it may sometimes be more merciful and loving to end suffering than to extend a joyless, unendurable life.

4. *When death becomes preferable to life, everyone would benefit if it were legal to show mercy.* Compassion and benevolence demand that we legalize assisted death for the sake of the afflicted and those who love them. The most powerful argument in favor of physician-assisted death comes from the families of those who have witnessed loved ones die in extreme agony. When medical science has done all it can and death has not yet brought merciful relief, family members suffer a sense of powerlessness and despair as they watch in horror someone they love dearly writhe in torment as they wait and hope for a quick end to their awful suffering. That these extreme cases are rare is indeed fortunate, but it does not render less important the appalling plight of whose who must live—hopeless and helpless—through such distress. It

would benefit everyone if choosing death in hopeless, intolerable situations were allowed under defined circumstances that prevent abuse.

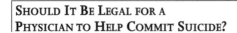

SHOULD IT BE LEGAL FOR A
PHYSICIAN TO HELP COMMIT SUICIDE?

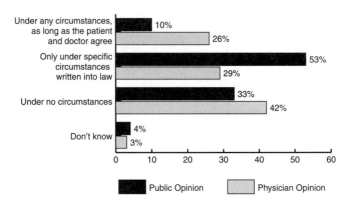

American Medical Association opinion survey, 1995.

The most forlorn of all are those who agonize over whether to take action in violation of the law to end the life of someone dear to them who pleads and prays for death. A few in desperation, unable to stand it any longer, take a gun or a pillow and do what they dread and hate to do but must do in order to bring relief to a parent or child or spouse who is glad for the intervention but is fearful of the legal consequences for those who have shown them mercy.

You have seen them, or heard them, or read about them. Their faces are sometimes hidden and their voices are disguised as they tell their sad stories. They must witness in secret to what has happened because the law condemns their compassion and calls them murderers. Yet they loved the deceased with all their hearts and were moved to do the dreadful deed out of pure benevolence.

THE DOCTRINE OF DOUBLE EFFECT

Physicians are more fortunate in that they can take refuge in the principle of the "double effect" and write on the death certificate the cause of death. Many of us have heard doctors report that they have, out of compassion and mercy, given heavy doses of morphine to relieve the intolerable distress of patients who are near to an inevitable death, knowing full well that the result will be to hasten the end. Somehow this is all right, since the primary aim is, we say, to relieve suffering and not to kill, but it would not be right, we are told, to do the very same thing with the primary aim of hastening death, while getting the secondary result of comfort.

Why do we force good people full of love, mercy, and compassion to such extreme measures to bring an end to hopeless torment when no cure or relief is possible for the dearest people on earth to them? Why do we force physicians to justify their mercy in hastening death by denying that they did it for that reason, when we all know what is really going on?

I am a theologian, a philosopher, an ethicist, and a Baptist minister. I hold our moral, legal, and theological heritage in high regard. But there are times when we need to rethink received wisdom by subjecting our principles, codes, and traditions to a fresh exposure to real life experience. Sometimes ideals that are designed to protect and enhance life may actually degrade life and be the source of unnecessary suffering. So it is I believe with the prohibition of physician-assisted death under any and all circumstances. We can provide an opportunity for patients in certain extreme and rare cases under strictly regulated conditions to manage their dying without endangering our reverence for life. In so doing we can provide a way to be merciful to the dying without branding those who show mercy as criminals. We can avoid the agony of family members and of physicians who must do in secret what love and compassion urge upon them and thus serve the dying while honoring the living.

"Physician-assisted suicide and euthanasia violate values that are fundamental to the practice of medicine and to the patient-physician relationship."

ASSISTED SUICIDE IS NOT AN ETHICALLY ACCEPTABLE PRACTICE FOR PHYSICIANS

Lonnie R. Bristow

Lonnie R. Bristow is former president of the American Medical Association, and the following viewpoint is excerpted from testimony she gave before the House of Representatives on the AMA's behalf. In it, Bristow argues that physician-assisted suicide constitutes a violation of medical ethics and threatens the doctor-patient relationship. However, she emphasizes the AMA's support for a patient's right to refuse treatment and a doctor's duty to prescribe adequate pain medication even if there is a risk that such medication might hasten death.

As you read, consider the following questions:

1. What is a physician's primary obligation, in Bristow's opinion?
2. Which two states does Bristow say have developed clear legislative guidance that can resolve most physicians' concerns about prescribing large amounts of pain medication?
3. According to the author, what reasons do patients cite for requesting physician-assisted suicide?

Excerpted from Lonnie R. Bristow's testimony before the U.S. House of Representatives, Committee on the Judiciary, Subcommittee on the Constitution, April 26, 1996. (The section of this testimony regarding education of physicians and patients has been deleted from this reprint.)

For nearly 2,500 years, physicians have vowed to "give no deadly drug if asked for it, [nor] make a suggestion to this effect." What has changed, that there should be this attempt to make "assisted suicide" an accepted practice of medicine? Certainly the experience of physical pain has not changed over time. Yet the blessings of medical research and technology present their own new challenges, as our ability to delay or draw out the dying process alters our perceptions and needs.

Our efforts in this new paradigm must recognize the importance of care that relieves pain, supports family and relationships, enhances functioning, and respects spiritual needs. Calls for legalization of physician-assisted suicide point to a public perception that these needs are not being met by the current health care system. In addition, society has not met its responsibility to plan adequately for end-of-life care. It is this issue— how to provide quality care at the end of life—which the AMA believes should be our legitimate focus.

THE POSITION OF THE AMERICAN MEDICAL ASSOCIATION

The AMA believes that physician-assisted suicide is unethical and fundamentally inconsistent with the pledge physicians make to devote themselves to healing and to life. Laws that sanction physician-assisted suicide undermine the foundation of the patient-physician relationship that is grounded in the patient's trust that the physician is working wholeheartedly for the patient's health and welfare. The multidisciplinary members of the New York State Task Force on Life and the Law concur in this belief, writing that "physician-assisted suicide and euthanasia violate values that are fundamental to the practice of medicine and the patient-physician relationship."

Yet physicians also have an ethical responsibility to relieve pain and to respect their patient's wishes regarding care, and it is when these duties converge at the bedside of a seriously or terminally ill patient that physicians are torn.

The AMA believes that these additional ethical duties require physicians to respond aggressively to the needs of the patients at the end of life with adequate pain control, emotional support, comfort care, respect for patient autonomy and good communications.

Further efforts are necessary to better educate physicians in the areas of pain management and effective end-of-life care. Patient education is the other essential component of an effective outreach to minimize the circumstances which might lead to a patient's request for physician-assisted suicide: inadequate social support; the perceived burden to family and friends; clinical depression; hopelessness; loss of self-esteem; and the fear of living with chronic, unrelieved pain.

ETHICAL CONSIDERATIONS

Physicians' Fundamental Obligation: The physician's primary obligation is to advocate for the individual patient. At the end of life, this means the physician must strive to understand the various existential, psychological, and physiological factors that play out over the course of terminal illness and must help the patient cope with each of them. Patients who are understandably apprehensive or afraid of their own mortality need support and comforting, not a prescription to help them avoid the issues of death. Patients who believe sudden and "controlled" death would protect them from the perceived indignities of prolonged deterioration and terminal illness must receive social support as well as the support of the profession to work through these issues. Providing assisted suicide would breach the ethical means of medicine to safeguard patients' dignity and independence.

Pain Management and the Doctrine of Double Effect: Many proponents of assisted suicide cite a fear of prolonged suffering and unmanageable pain as support for their position. For most patients, advancements in palliative care can adequately control pain through oral medications, nerve blocks or radiotherapy. We all recognize, however, that there are patients whose intractable pain cannot be relieved by treating the area, organ or system perceived as the source of the pain. For patients for whom pain cannot be controlled by other means, it is ethically permissible for physicians to administer sufficient levels of controlled substances to ease pain, even if the patient's risk of addiction or death is increased.

The failure of most states to expressly permit this practice has generated reluctance among physicians to prescribe adequate pain medication. Additional uncertainty is produced by the potential for legal action against the physician when controlled substances are prescribed in large amounts to treat patients with intractable pain. This uncertainty chills physicians' ability to effectively control their terminally ill patients' pain and suffering through the appropriate prescription and administration of opiates and other controlled substances. In this area, states such as California and Texas have developed clear legislative guidance that resolves these concerns for most physicians. The AMA is developing similarly structured model legislation for state medical societies to pursue with their state legislatures and medical licensing boards.

In some instances, administration of adequate pain medication will have the secondary effect of suppressing the respiration of the patient, thereby hastening death. This is commonly referred to as the "double effect." The distinction between this action and assisted suicide is crucial. The physician has an obligation to provide for the comfort of the patient. If there are no alternatives but to increase the risk of death in order to provide that comfort, the physician is ethically permitted to exercise that option. In this circumstance, the physician's clinical decision is guided by the intent to provide pain relief, rather than an intent to cause death. This distinguishes the ethical use of palliative care medications from the unethical application of medical skills to cause death.

A CRUCIAL DISTINCTION

Distinction Between Withholding or Withdrawing Treatment and Assisted Suicide: Some participants in the debate about assisted suicide see no meaningful distinction between withholding or withdrawing treatment and providing assistance in suicide. They argue that the results of each action are the same and therefore the acts themselves carry equal moral status. This argument largely ignores the distinction between act and omission in the circumstances of terminal care and does not address many of the principles that underlie the right of patients to refuse the continuation of medical care and the duty of physicians to exercise their best clinical judgment.

Specifically, proponents who voice this line of reasoning fail to recognize the crucial difference between a patient's right to refuse unwanted medical treatment and any proposed right to receive medical intervention which would cause death. Withholding or withdrawing treatment allows death to proceed naturally, with the underlying disease being the cause of death. Assisted suicide, on the other hand, requires action to cause death, independent from the disease process.

ASSISTED SUICIDE IN PRACTICE

The "Slippery Slope": Physician-assisted suicide raises troubling and insurmountable "slippery slope" problems. Despite attempts by some, it is difficult to imagine adequate safeguards which could effectively guarantee that patients' decisions to request assisted suicide were unambivalent, informed and free of coercion.

A policy allowing assisted suicide could also result in the victimization of poor and disenfranchised populations who may have greater financial burdens and social burdens which could be "relieved" by hastening death. As reported in 1994 by the New York State Task Force on Life and the Law (composed of bioethicists, lawyers, clergy and state health officials), "assisted suicide and euthanasia will be practiced through the prism of social inequality and prejudice that characterizes the delivery of services in all segments of society, including health care."

Studies documenting reasons for patient requests for physician-assisted suicide speak to our "slippery slope" concerns. Patients were rarely suffering intractable pain. Rather, they cited fears of losing control, being a burden, being dependent on others for personal care and loss of dignity often associated with end-stage disease.

Tony Auth © The Philadelphia Inquirer. Reprinted with permission of Universal Press Syndicate. All rights reserved.

The Case of the Netherlands: While euthanasia and assisted suicide are not legal in the Netherlands, comprehensive guidelines have been established which allow physicians to avoid prosecution for the practice. Despite this environment, Dutch physicians have become uneasy about their active role in euthanasia, prompting the Royal Dutch Medical Association to revise its recommendations on the practice.

Findings of more than 1,000 cases of involuntary euthanasia in the Netherlands should raise hackles in the United States, particularly given the stark societal differences between the two countries. Health coverage is universal in the Netherlands, the prevalence of long-term patient-physician relationships is greater and social supports are more comprehensive. The inequities in the American healthcare system, where the majority of patients who request physician-assisted suicide cite financial burden as a motive, make the practice of physician-assisted suicide all the more unjustifiable. No other country in the world, including the Netherlands, has legalized assisted suicide or euthanasia. This is one movement in which the United States should not be a "leader.". . .

A SIGN OF FAILURE

The movement for legally sanctioning physician-assisted suicide is a sign of society's failure to address the complex issues raised at the end of life. It is not a victory for personal rights. We are equipped with the tools to effectively manage end-of-life pain and to offer terminally ill patients dignity and to add value to their remaining time. As the voice of the medical profession, the AMA offers its capability to coordinate multidisciplinary discourse on end-of-life issues, for it is essential to coordinate medical educators, patients, advocacy organizations, allied health professionals and the counseling and pastoral professions to reach a comprehensive solution to these challenging issues. Our response should be a better informed medical profession and public, working together to preserve fundamental human values at the end of life.

"*A solid majority of practicing physicians believe in the need to alleviate pain and suffering under certain circumstances by hastening an approaching death.*"

PHYSICIANS SHOULD BE LEGALLY PERMITTED TO ASSIST IN SUICIDE

Derek Humphry and Mary Clement

In the following viewpoint, excerpted from their book *Freedom to Die: People, Politics, and the Right-to-Die Movement*, Derek Humphry and Mary Clement argue that current prohibitions on physician-assisted suicide (PAS) force many doctors to break the law in order to help their terminally ill patients to die. Much of the opposition to legalizing PAS, say the authors, comes from organized medicine, particularly the American Medical Association. The authors believe the AMA's position is grounded in a misguided interpretation of the Hippocratic Oath, which they contend is outdated. Derek Humphry is the founder of both the Hemlock Society and the Euthanasia Guidance and Research Organization, and Mary Clement is president of Gentle Closure, Inc., an organization that assists people in addressing end-of-life concerns. For more information, visit www.finalexit.org.

As you read, consider the following questions:

1. What popular maxim does not appear in the Hippocratic Oath, according to the authors?
2. What is the version of the Hippocratic Oath that has been endorsed by the World Medical Association known as?
3. According to Humphry and Clement, what percent of the nation's doctors support aid in dying?

S ome physicians are helping their patients achieve a dignified death with a lethal prescription or injection despite the law. The risks are high. Legal and professional pressures require the procedure to be carried out covertly. Patients fear involuntary commitment to prevent their suicides, and physicians fear criminal prosecution. Doctors rarely seek advice from colleagues, forgoing valuable information and support. The situation also forces many patients to conspire with their loved ones, who have reason to fear prosecution as a result of their assistance in the death.

THE COURAGE OF THEIR CONVICTIONS

Many doctors have the courage of their convictions, and risk loss of license, career, income, and personal freedom. A study showed that 16 percent of physicians polled in Washington State reported having been asked by their terminally ill patients for either physician-assisted suicide (PAS) or euthanasia. Of the patients who requested PAS, 24 percent received prescriptions, and of those who requested euthanasia, another 24 percent received lethal injections.

A study of Michigan oncologists reported that 18 percent of those who responded reported active participation in PAS; 4 percent reported participation in voluntary euthanasia: That is a total of 22 percent of Michigan's oncologists surveyed who complied with requests to hasten death. In another study of cancer specialists, 57 percent had been asked for help in ending their life, and 13.5 percent of them had complied.

People with AIDS often attempt suicide, and doctors appear increasingly willing to help them. More than half (53 percent) of San Francisco AIDS doctors surveyed admitted having helped at least one patient commit suicide. One doctor admitted to having assisted one hundred patients. "Everyone knows this occurs," says Thomas Mitchell, a public health specialist.

These figures show the high percentage of physicians who operate outside the law and the purview of the national and state medical organizations. The conventional wisdom that the American Medical Association (AMA) is "against assisted dying" belies the number of health care professionals who disagree enough with the law and the AMA to risk being charged with murder.

THREE CATEGORIES OF PHYSICIANS

Physicians fall into basically three categories, claims a *New England Journal of Medicine* editorial. Those in the category that supports the practice of hastening a death see it as a "compassionate response to a medical need, a symbol of nonabandonment, and a means to reestablish patients' trust in doctors who have used technology excessively. They argue that regulation of physician-assisted suicide is possible and, in fact, necessary to control the actions of physicians who are currently providing assistance surreptitiously."

The two remaining groups of physicians oppose legalization. One group is not ethically, morally, or religiously opposed to the practice and views it, in fact, as justifiable under certain circumstances—even participating in the practice. However, these physicians do not want it legalized and thus regulated. The third group, including the AMA, is morally opposed to hastening death. They believe physicians should not be executioners— should not endorse justified killing. . . .

OBJECTIONS TO PHYSICIAN-ASSISTED SUICIDE

Why is the medical establishment so averse to PAS when so many of its members favor it? Its history is to resist change, but what is the reasoning on this issue? What is it so afraid of?

Some doctors automatically object for religious reasons. There is also the generic concern that voluntary PAS will progress to eventually include killing people against their wishes or without their consent. Other than these general concerns, the most frequently raised objections are: (1) pressure would be put on elderly and infirm patients by family members who do not want the burden but do want the inheritance; (2) there would be reduced incentive to improve palliative care, especially pain control; (3) helping patients die would taint the integrity of the medical profession; (4) ignorance of effective methods might lead to botched suicide attempts; (5) the practice would be dangerous for patients with undiagnosed depression; (6) it is unethical for physicians to hasten death or actively participate in the killing of patients; (7) doctors are healers, not murderers; and (8) the practice would destroy the "trust factor" of the doctor-patient relationship.

THE HIPPOCRATIC OATH

The all-encompassing reason most frequently offered, however, is that any assistance on the part of the doctor in hastening a patient's death is in violation of the ethics and tradition of the medical profession. To this end the Hippocratic Oath is often cited. Yet the Oath has been selectively cited over time both in support for and against the matter.

The Oath of Hippocrates reads as follows:

> I swear by Apollo Physician and Asclepius and Hygeia and Panacea and all the gods and goddesses, making them my wit-

ness, that I will fulfill according to my ability and judgment this oath and this covenant:

To hold him who has taught me this art as equal to my parents and to live my life in partnership with him, and if he is in need of money to give him a share of mine, and to regard his off-spring as equal to my brothers in male lineage and to teach them this art—if they desire to learn it—without fee and covenant; to give a share of precepts and oral instruction and all the other learning to my sons and to the sons of him who has instructed me and to pupils who have signed the covenant and have taken an oath according to the medical law, but to no one else.

I will apply dietetic measures for the benefit of the sick according to my ability and judgment; I will keep them from harm and injustice.

I will neither give a deadly drug to anybody if asked for it, nor will I make a suggestion to this effect. Similarly, I will not give to a woman an abortion remedy. In purity and holiness I will guard my life and my art.

Whatever house I may visit, I will come for the benefit of the sick, remaining free of all intentional injustice, of all mischief and in particular sexual relations with both female and male persons, be they free or slaves.

Whatever I may see or hear in the course of treatment in regard to the life of men, which on no account one must spread abroad, I will keep to myself holding such things shameful to be spoken about.

If I fulfill this oath and do not violate it, may it be granted to me to enjoy life and art, being honored with fame among all men for all time to come; if I transgress it and swear falsely, may the opposite of all this be my lot.

MISCONCEPTIONS ABOUT THE OATH

Conventional wisdom says that physicians are bound by the Hippocratic Oath. This is not the case. It is ironic that the profession, which prides itself on the Oath, does not require its members to take it. Indeed, physicians who have actually taken it are few and far between. Many physicians have never even read it, much less sworn to it. Few medical schools require its reading at graduation ceremonies. At the most, and even this is uncommon, medical school commencements include a rote and ritualistic recitation of the Oath, but it is usually a sanitized version that [, writes Jonathan D. Moreno in his book *Arguing Euthanasia*,] "omits references to sensitive subjects like euthanasia and abortion. Ignorance of the Hippocratic Oath's actual content is perhaps best exemplified by the frequent references to the maxim *Primum non nocere,* or 'First do no harm.' The precept is indeed Hippocratic, but it does not appear in the Oath."

Those who argue against physician assistance quote the phrase, "I will neither give a deadly drug to anyone, if asked for, nor will I make a suggestion to this effect." It also forbids performing an abortion, receiving money for teaching medicine and performing surgery. What makes all the difference, and what is frequently overlooked, is that the Oath's first sentence affords room for "ability and judgment."

DOES ASSISTED DYING VIOLATE MEDICAL TRADITION?

There is no such thing as a linear medical "tradition" that has been handed down over thousands of years. Each new generation of physicians has reinterpreted this ethos for themselves, influenced by social conditions and technological changes. . . .

Earlier in this century, the ethos of medicine moved swiftly in the direction of prolonging life as a result of advances in medical technology. This technological ability to keep patients alive, even against their will or when they're in persistent vegetative states, has led to numerous court cases and legislation over the past twenty years on behalf of patients' rights. In addition, these legal actions have been followed in the past few years by reversals in hospital policies of just a decade ago regarding the use of cardiopulmonary resuscitation. As a result, do-not-resuscitate (DNR) orders by physicians are becoming commonplace. And though physicians cannot legally "help patients die," they can—and frequently do—"allow patients to die," even mentally incompetent patients, by withholding and withdrawing life-sustaining treatments, including artificial nutrition and hydration. These various changes clearly show that the ethos of medicine is not something that has remained the same even during the past fifty years. Now the question to be asked is whether the ethos will change further to recognize that more harm may be done favoring a slow and agonizing death for a patient than following a patient's desire to alleviate suffering quickly and gently with assistance from a physician.

Stephen Jamison, *Final Acts of Love: Families, Friends, and Assisted Dying,* 1995.

It is thus more of a guiding tradition to provide ethical guidelines than a literal promise to do or not do something. Physicians are free to rely on their own interpretation of the Oath—if they choose to rely on it at all. An elderly physician who had taken the life of a dying patient the previous day with an injection of morphine had this to say about his actions: "I don't believe I broke my Hippocratic Oath. Part of that Oath is not to do any harm to people and try to help people. I thought I was not doing harm but good in this case. I thought it was colleagues who were doing harm in prolonging his pain and suffering. The Hippocratic Oath in spirit is what I was doing. It will depend on your interpretation."

LITTLE RELEVANCE TODAY

Except in its broadest sense, the Oath has little relevance today. "A literal interpretation of the Hippocratic Oath in the twentieth century would be contrary to the very principle of application of fact that was so important to Hippocrates," writes John H. Leversee, physician and author of *Hippocrates Revisited: A View from General Practice*. "Time does change most things, if not all things. The passage of twenty-four centuries certainly changes the circumstances under which one must interpret facts. . . . Thus, it seems to me, we must see his principles in their broadest sense and not be bogged down by literal interpretations."

By 1948 the World Medical Association (WMA) issued a more current version of the Oath. It became known as the Geneva version of the Hippocratic Oath, or the Geneva Oath, because leaders of the medical profession accepted it at a meeting in Geneva. It contains no direct reference to abortion, to surgery, to payment, to educating the children of one's teachers or to assisting in a suicide. The revised Oath reads:

> Now being admitted to the profession of medicine, I solemnly pledge to consecrate my life to the services of humanity. I will give respect and gratitude to my teachers. I will practice medicine with conscience and dignity. The health and life of my patient will be my first consideration. I will hold in confidence all that my patient confides in me.

> I will maintain the honor and the noble traditions of the medical profession. My colleagues will be as my brothers. I will not permit consideration of race, religion, nationality, party politics or social standing to intervene between my duty and my patient. I will maintain the utmost respect for human life from the time of conception. Even under threat I will not use my knowledge contrary to the laws of humanity.

> These promises I make freely and upon my honor.

Physicians opposed to PAS ignore the existence of the Geneva Oath. They quote the 2,500-year-old version, even though the WMA has deemed it outdated. Nevertheless the original version serves as a convenient justification to support the claim that an assisted death should remain prohibited. It is similar to quoting a legal decision that was subsequently overturned by a higher court, knowing that the public is not sophisticated enough to see through the deception. An even more updated version of the Oath is under consideration by the WMA. There is no reason to expect, however, that selective reference to the ancient Oath will cease as long as it substantiates what benefits the physician.

DOCTORS WANT TO RETAIN CONTROL

There exists a truth far more subtle than the party-line talk of legalization's endangering patients and violating health care's mission to heal. The public debate obscures private concerns about legalization: regulations, red tape, and loss of control, which is, perhaps, the real issue here. Legalization would give patients more control, as Quinlan and its progeny empowered the patient—a fact the profession still resents. Measures 16 and 51 in Oregon were about the empowerment of patients, not doctors. The initiatives were fueled by the realization that physicians often ignore patient end-of-life wishes and appear uninterested in dealing with patient pain and emotional issues.

Charles Baron, professor of constitutional law and bioethics at the Boston College Law School, explains that physicians are concerned that legalizing assisted suicide would lead to stricter oversight of other end-of-life decisions, such as removing patients from ventilators. "I think it is truly motivated by the fear that doctors will lose their totally unsupervised autonomy when it comes to making decisions about their patients."

THE HARD LINE

While struggling to retain some control, the AMA knows that its public and private image needs improvement. Membership is dropping. In the beginning of 1997 the association represented just under 40 percent of the nation's 700,000 physicians, down from 51 percent nine years earlier, and down from its high of 75 percent in the 1960s. Being so out of sync with physicians over current issues, such as physician participation in the death of a terminal patient, contributes to its immateriality. The AMA's irrelevancy has hurt it badly; membership dues dropped $2.1 million from 1995 to 1996, a shortfall of $1.3 million.

The medical establishment is beginning to concede physician assistance in dying. Similar to the way in which it eventually agreed to living wills, women surgeons, Red Cross blood banks, and Medicare, this compliance has not been voluntary or without a fight. The Oregon Medical Association, the organization that remained neutral for the first Oregon initiative, but then opposed the practice in the 1997 initiative, is cooperating with the state's new law—even if without enthusiasm.

Faced with mounting evidence that PAS will one day be legal throughout the nation, other regional medical communities are taking tentative steps toward setting professional standards for helping people die. The Michigan State Medical Society, a group of California health care providers, and Stanford University Center for Biomedical Ethics are working independently on proper ways to handle patients who want to die.

The AMA, however, continues to take a hard line. Dr. Charles Plows, chairman of the AMA's Council on Ethical and Judicial Affairs, said after a recent meeting, "We did talk about it, and decided this was not the proper time to consider guidelines. My own opinion is if we produce guidelines, we are indirectly offering some credence to physician-assisted suicide. It gives more fuel to the fire."

Bioethicist Arthur Caplan reacts to Plows's and the AMA's ostrich approach to the growing issue: "Dr. Plows is, if not standing in front of a steamroller, he's at least got a rapidly moving train headed straight at him. I'm on his side. I oppose legalization right now. But I believe if you can't win your argument, your next obligation is to make sure as few people as possible get hurt."

Change Is Inevitable

It has been said that the dinosaur became extinct because it could not adjust to a changing environment. Only time will tell if the same adage holds true for the medical establishment. Instead of being in the forefront of implementing workable guidelines for the inevitable legalization, the AMA is fighting fiercely to maintain its diminished reputation and authority.

By contrast a solid majority of practicing physicians believe in the need to alleviate pain and suffering under certain circumstances by hastening an approaching death. A substantial number practice what they believe, at considerable risk. Unfortunately this polarization will make it difficult to reach a consensus that will benefit the American people. Yet with 60 percent of the nation's doctors supporting aid in dying, they join the rest of the communities struggling to cope with societal changes that are overwhelming resistance to assisted suicide.

In a rare strand of liberal thinking, the usually conservative *British Medical Journal* has praised the renegade, Doctor Kevorkian, as a "medical hero." It quotes the *Oxford English Dictionary*: "A hero is a man of action rather than thought and lives by a personal code of honour that admits of no qualification. His responses are usually instinctive, predictable and inevitable. He accepts challenge and sometimes even courts disaster." To be a hero, the *Journal* continues, "means being honest with yourself and acting on your own morality, risking the fall from the pinnacle." The health care professionals who confront the issues, take the risks, and attempt to stop the hypocrisy are the real heroes of today's right-to-die movement. Meanwhile the AMA complacently issues press releases, attempts to polish its tarnished image, and struggles to maintain the status quo, with apparent dismissal of the inevitable.

"The state has a powerful interest in preventing the healing profession from becoming also the death-dealing profession."

PHYSICIANS SHOULD NOT BE LEGALLY PERMITTED TO ASSIST IN SUICIDE

Leon R. Kass and Nelson Lund

In the following viewpoint, Leon Kass and Nelson Lund contend that ethical and legal prohibitions on physician-assisted suicide (PAS) are the best way to ensure that physicians do not abuse the practice. Kass and Lund argue that the Hippocratic Oath, which they believe forbids PAS, serves as an important reminder to physicians of the power they have over their patients. In the authors' view, legalizing PAS, and abandoning the Hippocratic Oath, would weaken the guidelines that help doctors separate their personal judgments from what is best for their patients. Leon Kass is a physician and a professor at the University of Chicago, and Nelson Lund is a political scientist and a professor at the George Mason University School of Law.

As you read, consider the following questions:

1. According to Kass and Lund, why did Hippocratic physicians voluntarily set limits on their own conduct?
2. In the authors' view, why are medical students, interns, and residents taught a "profound repugnance for medical killing"?
3. Why is the principle of double effect important, in the authors' view?

Excerpted from Leon R. Kass and Nelson Lund, "Courting Death: Assisted Suicide, Doctors, and the Law," Commentary, December 1996. Reprinted by permission; all rights reserved.

Authorizing physician-assisted suicide would . . . overturn a centuries-old taboo against medical killing, a taboo understood by many to be one of the cornerstones of the medical ethic. This taboo is at least as old as, and is most famously formulated in, the Hippocratic Oath, where it stands as the first negative promise of professional self-restraint: "I will neither give a deadly drug to anybody if *asked for it*, nor will I make a suggestion to this effect. . . . In purity and holiness I will guard my life and my art." This clearly is a pledge to refrain from practicing euthanasia, even on request, and from assisting or even encouraging a willing patient in suicide.

This self-imposed professional forbearance, which was not required by the Greek laws or customs of the time, is rooted in deep insights into the nature of medicine. First, it recognizes the dangerous moral neutrality of medical technique: drugs can both cure and kill. Only if the means used serve a professionally appropriate end will medical practice be ethical. Accordingly, the Oath rules out assisting in suicide because the end that medical technique properly serves—the wholeness and well-working of the living human body—would be contradicted should the physician engage in delivering death-dealing drugs or advice.

Second, and most important, the taboo against euthanasia and assisted suicide—like the taboos against violating patient confidentiality and against sexual misconduct, enunciated later in the Oath—addresses a prominent "occupational hazard" to which the medical professional is especially prone: a temptation to take advantage of the vulnerability and exposure that the practice of medicine requires of patients. Just as patients necessarily divulge to the physician private and intimate details of their personal lives, and necessarily expose their naked bodies to the physician's objectifying gaze and investigating hands, so they necessarily expose and entrust the care of their very lives to the physician's skill, technique, judgment, and character. Mindful of the meaning of such exposure and vulnerability, and mindful too of their own human penchant for error and mischief, Hippocratic physicians voluntarily set limits on their own conduct, pledging not to take advantage of or to violate the patient's intimacies, naked sexuality, or life itself.

A Document for All Times and Places

The ancient Hippocratic physicians' refusal to assist in suicide was not part of an aggressive, so-called "vitalist" approach to dying patients or an unwillingness to accept mortality. On the contrary, understanding well the limits of the medical art, they refused to intervene aggressively when the patient was deemed incurable, and they regarded it as inappropriate to prolong the natural process of dying when death was unavoidable. Insisting on the moral importance of distinguishing between letting die (often not only permissible but laudatory) and actively causing death (impermissible), they protected themselves and their patients from their own possible weaknesses and folly, thereby preserving the moral integrity ("the purity and holiness") of their art and profession.

That the Oath and its ethical vision of medicine is the product of classical Greek antiquity reminds us that the ban on physician-assisted suicide was not and is not the result of religious impulses alone. The Oath is fundamentally pagan and medical, and it has no connection with biblical religion or the Judeo-Christian doctrines of the sanctity of human life. Nor is the Oath merely a parochial product of ancient Greek culture. Notwithstanding the fact that it begins by invoking Apollo and other deities no longer worshiped, it reflects and articulates a coherent, rational, and indeed wise, vision of the art of medicine. That is why it has been widely accepted in the West as a document for all times and places.

PHYSICIAN PARTICIPATION IN ABORTIONS

The Hippocratic Oath also proscribes physician participation in abortions. Before *Roe v. Wade*, this taboo governed American medical practice, but it has since fallen away. For this reason, some commentators dismiss the Hippocratic Oath as passé, and regard its proscription of assisting suicide as irrelevant to our morally more pluralistic times. The Ninth Circuit, for example, asserted that after *Roe*, "doctors began performing abortions routinely and the ethical integrity of the medical profession remained undiminished." But the court cited no evidence to support this cheery conclusion, and there are, in fact, grounds to argue the contrary. Massive numbers of abortions are now being performed, far beyond what was originally expected, and for reasons not originally regarded as appropriate. Moreover, physician acceptance of abortion may be partly responsible for recent weakenings in the profession's aversion to causing death, seen in those physicians who are today willing to practice euthanasia, a majority of whom have entered the profession since *Roe*. Indeed, one of the arguments offered 25 years ago against allowing doctors to perform abortions was that it would inevitably lead to doctors performing euthanasia. More than halfway down that slippery slope, it should be considered an open question, to say the least, whether the ethical integrity of the medical profession has "remained undiminished."

Be that as it may, the taboo against medical killing and death-dealing is not tied solely to the venerable but now partly compromised Hippocratic Oath. The proscription has been reaffirmed in numerous professional codes and statements of principle. The American Medical Association's code of Medical Ethics, for example, very explicitly rules out physician-assisted suicide, on the grounds that it is "fundamentally incompatible with the physician's role as healer, would be difficult or impossible to control, and would pose serious societal risks." The AMA's policy statements have repeatedly reiterated this position.

ABANDONING THE OATH?

Some now choose to characterize these teachings as merely the residue of tradition, and to argue that times have changed. The received wisdom of the medical profession, never mind Hippocrates, is not wisdom for today, they contend. Today, patients die differently, the vast majority in institutions, and most deaths are connected with some decision about withholding or withdrawing technological intervention. Our population is now aged and suffers increasingly from chronic and degenerative diseases and dementias. The cost of medical care is extremely high, especially for persons in the last year of life. Many people fear an overmedicalized death and a protracted process of dying, made possible by new technological devices such as respirators, defibrillators, dialyzers, and devices for artificial feeding.

Suicide was decriminalized long ago, and we have recognized the importance of patient autonomy in medical decision-making, especially at the end of life. We have established clear legal rights to refuse and to discontinue medical intervention, even should death be a likely outcome. Living wills and advance directives to protect our wishes should we fall incompetent have legal force in nearly every state. But although the hospice movement and advances in pain control already make physically comfortable dying possible for most people, some still want the right to have medical assistance in committing suicide and also direct killing by physicians. Public-opinion polls, though they should be viewed with caution, appear to indicate support for such a right. Moreover, many doctors are apparently willing not only to accede to requests for deadly drugs, but also to administer them to patients unable to take them for themselves. Some physicians, it is alleged, are already doing so in secret.

In short, so the argument goes, the ancient taboo against

physician-assisted suicide and euthanasia is now an obstacle to a humane death. What would be lost if the taboo fell?

The answer is that a great deal would be lost. . . .

Among its major purposes, medical ethics seeks to protect physicians against both their strengths and their weaknesses. To protect against the danger of professional arrogance, physicians are taught about the need for humility concerning the limits of their own specialized competencies and their ability to offer precise prognoses or to effect permanent cures. They are warned against prideful overconfidence and the belief that they always know better what is in the patient's best interest. They are taught to seek outside consultation, to be modest in their predictions and promises, to secure informed consent for all procedures, and to respect their patients' prerogatives in refusing treatment or hospitalization. They gradually, and no doubt imperfectly, learn how limited is their ability to preserve health, prolong life, and forestall death.

Perhaps even more important are those aspects of medical ethics that protect the physician against his ordinary human weaknesses: his tendency to allow his own self-interest (regarding time, money, or competing concerns) to undermine his devotion to his patients' needs; his own distastes, dislikes, and frustrations regarding difficult or incurable patients, any of which might lead him to shortchange their care, to become indifferent to their needs and complaints, or even to neglect and abandon them outright; his own fear of death, which might prevent him from allowing his patients to die without added indignities. All these lessons are very difficult to learn and faithfully practice, for taking care of the sick and, especially, the dying places extraordinary and unrelenting demands on one's patience, equanimity, and strength of character.

PROTECTING PHYSICIANS FROM THEMSELVES

Despite the medical ideal, and despite all exhortations to the contrary, physicians do in fact get tired of treating patients who are hard to cure, who resist their best efforts, who are on their way down—especially when they have had no long-term relationship with them over many years. "Gorks," "gomers," and "vegetables" are only some of the less-than-affectionate names such patients receive from interns and residents. Once the venerable taboo against assisted suicide and medical killing is broken, many physicians will be much less able to care wholeheartedly for these patients.

With death now a legitimate "therapeutic option," the exhausted medical resident will be tempted to find it the best treatment for the little old lady "dumped" again on the emergency room by the nearby nursing home. Should she get the necessary penicillin and respirator one more time, or, perhaps, this time just an overdose of morphine? Even if the morphine is not given, the thinkability of doing so, and the likely impossibility of discovery and prosecution, will greatly alter the physician's attitude toward his patients. Today, hospital patients whose charts contain "Do Not Resuscitate" orders are very often treated differently from the rest. This happens not because of official policy, but despite it. A subtle message is silently conveyed that such patients are less worthy of continued life. Should lethal

THE POWER OF TRADITION

In stating that "the Oath has little relevance today," [Derek Humphry and Mary Clement] reveal a basic misunderstanding of its importance in defining just what the practice of medicine is all about.

When the two authors erroneously write that "the profession, which prides itself on the Oath, does not require its members to take it," they are attempting to support their contention that its proscription against helping a patient to his death is "outdated," and therefore no longer valid. They decry the way in which medical groups trot out its sonorous phrases when seeking grounds on which to campaign against physician-assisted suicide, though it is common knowledge (or so they state) that the ancient pledge has no claim on the ethics of a modern physician. Yet Humphry and Clement are sorrily misinformed. . . .

The Oath is a symbolic declaration linking all physicians of all times in the common understanding that henceforth their lives are to be consecrated to the care of the sick. In a slick and materialistic era such as our own, talk of consecration may seem melodramatic to some. But others will recognize the power of feeling that such a sentiment arouses in a young physician. Many doctors are sustained for decades by that feeling of hallowed duty, amid the vicissitudes of the difficult and sometimes discouraging sequence of illness-experiences that we call a career. The power of tradition is one of the factors that bind us together not only as a profession, but also as a calling. It signifies that a shared moral code exists, from which none of us is exempt. Though we may differ about some of its elements, the existence of such a code pervades and enriches the atmosphere in which we care for our patients.

Sherwin B. Nuland, New Republic, November 2, 1998.

drugs become a legal option, such psychological changes in physicians will be even more difficult to resist. And the consequences will often be deadly.

Even the most humane and conscientious physician psychologically needs protection against himself and his weaknesses if he is to care fully for those who entrust themselves to him. One physician who has worked for many years in a hospice caring for dying patients put the matter most convincingly: "Only because I knew that I could not and would not kill my patients was I able to enter most fully and intimately into caring for them as they lay dying."

PRIVATE PREJUDICES VERSUS PROFESSIONAL CONDUCT
The taboo against physician-assisted suicide is perhaps even more crucial as a protection against physicians' arrogance—their willingness to judge, on the basis of their own private prejudices and attitudes, whether this or that life is unworthy of continued existence. This most important point is generally overlooked in discussions of assisted suicide because so much attention is focused on the patient's voluntary request for death. But in order to comply with such a request, the physician must, willy-nilly, play the part of judge, and his judgments will be decidedly nonmedical and nonprofessional, based on his own personal standards. One will choose to assist death over against moderate or impending senility, another against paraplegia, a third against severe pain or blindness or prolonged depression. Only those requests resonating with the physician's own criteria of "intolerable" or "unworthy" lives will be honored.

The problem is not primarily that physicians believe some lives more worthy or better lived than others; nearly all people hold such opinions and make such judgments. The danger comes when they act on these judgments, and especially when they do so under the cloak of professional prestige and compassion. Medical ethics, mindful that medicine wields formidable powers over life and death, has for centuries prevented physicians from acting professionally on the basis of any such personal judgment. Medical students, interns, and residents are taught—and acquire—a profound repugnance to medical killing, as a major defense against committing, or even contemplating, the worst action to which their arrogance and/or their weaknesses might lead them.

At the same time, it is true, they are also taught not always to oppose death. Because it is part of life, physicians must not hate death as they abhor killing. They are taught—and it is a lesson not easily learned—when they should abandon interventions, cease interfering with the dying process, and give only care, comfort, and company to the dying patient. But in order to be able to keep their balance, physicians have insisted on the absolute distinction between letting die and deliberate killing. Nonmedical laymen (including lawyers and judges) may not be impressed with this distinction, but for practicing physicians it is morally crucial.

For one thing, death does not necessarily follow the discontinuance of treatment. Karen Ann Quinlan lived more than ten years after the courts allowed the "life-sustaining" respirator to be removed; not her physician but her underlying fatal illness became the true cause of her death. The result in the Quinlan case shows that the right to discontinue treatment cannot be part of some larger right, in the words of the Ninth Circuit Court of Appeals, to "determine the time and manner of one's own death." Indeed, it is both naive and thoughtless to believe that we can exercise such a "right" short of killing ourselves or arranging to be killed on schedule. The whole notion of the so-called right to die exposes the shallowness of our exaggerated belief in mastery over nature and fortune, a belief that informs the Ninth Circuit's opinion and, indeed, our entire technological approach to death.

What is most important *morally* is that the physician who ceases treatment does not intend the death of the patient. Even if death follows as a result of his action or omission, his intention is to avoid useless and degrading medical additions to the already sad end of a life. By contrast, in assisted suicide and all other forms of direct killing, the physician must necessarily and indubitably intend primarily that the patient be made dead. And he must knowingly and indubitably cast himself in the role of the agent of death. This remains true even if he is merely an assistant in suicide. Morally, a physician who provides the pills or lets the patient plunge the syringe after he leaves the room is no different from one who does the deed himself. As the Hippocratic Oath puts it, "I will neither give a deadly drug to anybody if asked for it, nor will I make a suggestion to this effect."

THE PRINCIPLE OF DOUBLE EFFECT

The same prohibition of physician killing continues to operate in other areas of palliative care where some have sought to deny its importance. For example, physicians often and quite properly prescribe high doses of narcotics to patients with widespread cancer in an effort to relieve severe pain, even though such medication carries an increased risk of death. But it is wrong to say that the current use of intravenous morphine in advanced cancer patients already constitutes a practice of medical killing. The physician here intends only the relief of suffering, which presupposes that the patient will continue to live in order to be relieved. Death, should it occur, is unintended and regretted.

The well-established rule of medical ethics that governs this practice is known as the principle of double effect, a principle misunderstood by the Ninth Circuit. It is morally licit to embrace a course of action that intends and serves a worthy goal (like relieving suffering), employing means that may have, as an unintended and undesired consequence, some harm or evil for the patient. Such cases are distinguished from the morally illicit efforts, like those of Jack Kevorkian, that indirectly "relieve suffering" by deliberately providing a lethal dose of a drug and thus eliminating the sufferer.

True, it may not always be easy to distinguish the two cases from the outside. When death occurs from respiratory depression following morphine administration, the outcome—a dead patient—is the same, and the proximate cause—morphine—may also be the same. Physical evidence alone, obtained after the fact, will often not be enough to tell us whether the physician acted with intent to ease pain or with intent to kill. But that is *exactly* why the principle of double effect is so important. Only an ethic opposing the intent to kill, which is reinforced by current laws, keeps the physician from such deliberate deadly acts.

Both as a matter of law and as a matter of medical ethics, the right to refuse unwanted medical intervention is properly seen not as part of a right to become dead but rather (like the rest of the doctrine of informed consent) as part of a right protecting how we choose to live, even while we are dying. What become unwanted treatments are first begun on the basis of a prudent judgment, weighing benefits and burdens and, in the event of doubt, usually erring on the side of life and hope for recovery. But after a proper trial, when recovery seems beyond reasonable possibility, and when the patient's condition deteriorates, one is medically and morally free to abandon the therapeutic efforts, even if death results. Yet it is not the intent of this discontinuance—whether by a physical act of omission or commission—that the patient become dead.

It is therefore false to say (as the Second Circuit Court of Appeals does) that physicians who turn off a respirator are already practicing assisted suicide, or (as the Ninth Circuit says) that physicians who today run increased risks of their patients' death in order to provide adequate pain medication are knowingly and intentionally killing them. No doubt, some physicians, already far down the slippery slope to involuntary euthanasia, may be abusing the principle of double effect, but such abuse in no way justifies blurring the only line that can be drawn clearly in this difficult area.

Law cannot substitute for medical ethics. It cannot teach or inculcate the right attitudes and standards that professionals need if they are to preserve the fragile moral integrity on which the proper practice of medicine depends. But the law can support that ethic by enacting and upholding a bright-line rule that coincides with the necessary prohibition against doctors becoming agents of death. Especially where there is grave doubt that adequate substitutes can be found for such a rule, or that there can be enforceable guidelines and safeguards for medical practice in its absence, the state has a powerful interest in preventing the healing profession from becoming also the death-dealing profession.

That many physicians are already tempted to assist in suicide, and to perform euthanasia, is not a reason for changing the traditional rule. On the contrary, it may very well be a warning of how weakened the fragile medical ethic has already become, and how important it is to help shore it up. Where our state governments have decided to uphold this ethic by proscribing assisted suicide, and where the authoritative voices of the medical profession urge them to continue to do so, federal courts should not be in the business of undermining their efforts.

It may seem paradoxical that we have been defending a law on the ground that it helps the people whose conduct it restricts to practice self-regulation. But this is exactly where law is often most important and useful. Under the growing economic, legal, and technologically driven pressures that trouble modern American medicine, it is increasingly difficult for the medical profession to uphold its own ethical standards and for individual physicians to keep their moral balance. Regarding no matter is it more important to maintain professional ethics than in the delicate and dangerous area of care for the dying. Regarding no matter is there greater danger to patients, physicians, and the whole fabric of their relationship.

State governments, recognizing the importance of medicine's moral standards in general and of the ancient taboo against medical killing in particular, have reasonably and rightfully elected to support the profession with laws banning all physician-assisted suicide. Far from being paradoxical, that is the course of wisdom.

PERIODICAL BIBLIOGRAPHY

The following articles have been selected to supplement the diverse views presented in this chapter. Addresses are provided for periodicals not indexed in the *Readers' Guide to Periodical Literature*, the *Alternative Press Index*, the *Social Sciences Index*, or the *Index to Legal Periodicals and Books*.

Congressional Digest	Special issue on physician-assisted suicide, November 1998.
Kathleen Marie Dixon	"The Quality of Mercy: Reflections on Provider-Assisted Suicide," *Journal of Clinical Ethics*, Fall 1997. Available from 107 E. Church St., Frederick, MD 21701.
Tom Duffy	"In the Name of Mercy," *People Weekly*, April 7, 1997.
Linda L. Emanuel	"Facing Requests for Physician-Assisted Suicide," *JAMA*, August 19, 1998. Available from PO Box 10946, Chicago, IL 60610-0946.
Jon Fuller	"Physician-Assisted Suicide: An Unnecessary Crisis," *America*, July 19, 1997.
James F. Keenan	"The Case for Physician-Assisted Suicide?" *America*, November 14, 1998.
Charles Krauthammer	"First and Last, Do No Harm: Allowing Doctors to Aid People in Committing Suicide Is Unconscionable," *Time*, April 15, 1996.
Paul R. McHugh	"The Kevorkian Epidemic," *American Scholar*, Winter 1997.
Robert B. Mellert	"Cure or Care? The Future of Medical Ethics," *Futurist*, July/August 1997.
Franklin G. Miller and Howard Brody	"Professional Integrity and Physician-Assisted Death," *Hastings Center Report*, May/June 1995.
Sherwin Nuland	"Doctors, Patients, and the End: The Right to Live," *New Republic*, November 2, 1998.
Shannon A. Thomas	"Physician-Assisted Suicide," *Commonweal*, June 1, 1996.
David C. Thomasma	"When Physicians Choose to Participate in the Death of Their Patients: Ethics and Physician-Assisted Suicide," *Journal of Law, Medicine & Ethics*, Fall 1996.
Louis Vernacchio	"Physician-Assisted Suicide: Reflections of a Young Doctor," *America*, August 31, 1996.

FOR FURTHER DISCUSSION

CHAPTER 1

1. One of the principal arguments for euthanasia, emphasized by Derek Humphry, is that individuals should have the right to choose the manner in which they die, regardless of other people's views about the morality of suicide or killing. Is euthanasia a personal decision, or do society and government have some right to regulate such decisions? Defend your answer.

2. Marcia Angell emphasizes another reason people support euthanasia, arguing that it is sometimes the most compassionate way to help terminally ill patients who are in severe pain. Do you find Angell's argument more or less convincing than Humphry's viewpoint emphasizing individual decision making? Why?

3. The viewpoints by the Michigan Catholic Conference and John Shelby Spong discuss euthanasia from similar religious perspectives, both accepting the premise that human life is sacred and should not be destroyed. However, Spong believes that "life must not be identified with the extension of biological assistance" while the Michigan Catholic Conference supports life "from the first moment of conception to our last natural breath." How do these differing views affect each author's position on euthanasia? In your opinion, must a euthanasia supporter reject the belief that human life is sacred, or are the two views compatible in some way? Explain your answer.

4. In her viewpoint, Marcia Angell contends that withdrawing treatment from a patient attached to a respirator is not a "passive" act, and would constitute murder if it was done against the wishes of the patient. John Shelby Spong asserts that the distinction between active and passive euthanasia "has been rendered all but meaningless by the advances in modern medicine." One implication of these claims is that if active euthanasia and the withdrawal of treatment are morally equivalent, then either both should be permitted or neither should. How does Daniel P. Sulmasy respond to this argument?

CHAPTER 2

1. Faye Girsh states that legalized physician aid-in-dying would be limited to the terminally ill. Why does Yale Kamisar believe that this limit would be legally unenforceable?

2. Yale Kamisar believes that although legalized euthanasia might help some individuals, it would have a negative effect on the way most terminally ill patients are treated. If euthanasia were legal, he says, weak and vulnerable patients would feel pressured to choose euthanasia, and people's overall respect for human life would be diminished. In contrast, Faye Girsh argues that legalizing physician aid-in-dying would have an overall positive effect, since it would benefit suffering patients, bring the practice out into the open, and allow it to be regulated. Which argument do you find most convincing? Do you think legalizing euthanasia would benefit, harm, or not affect most terminally ill patients? Defend your answer.

3. Activists on both sides of the euthanasia debate agree that patients at the end of their lives should have better access to quality hospice care. However, leaders within the hospice movement disagree as to whether the ethics of hospice care are compatible with assisted suicide. Why does Joe Loconte believe that hospice sets itself squarely against assisted death? What principle does Timothy Quill believe makes hospice compatible with physician aid-in-dying? Which author is more persuasive, and why?

CHAPTER 3

1. Opponents of euthanasia often argue that the dangers associated with legalizing voluntary euthanasia outweigh the benefits. In contrast to this risk-benefits approach, Gerald A. Larue places his faith in democracy, maintaining that Americans would not permit a shift from voluntary euthanasia to involuntary killing. James Thornton, however, believes that many Americans have lost moral direction, and that the slide down a "slippery slope" toward involuntary euthanasia is already underway. Which of the two viewpoints do you find most persuasive, and why?

2. Diane Coleman contends that people are more likely to condone euthanasia for the disabled. Do you believe that legalizing assisted suicide would pose a greater threat to the disabled than to other groups? Why or why not?

3. David Orentlicher outlines safeguards that he believes can prevent the abuse of physician-assisted suicide. Why does Herbert Hendin believe that such safeguards would be ineffective? Do you believe physician-assisted suicide can be effectively regulated?

4. Discussions of euthanasia in the Netherlands often mention the Remmelink report, the government-commissioned study

that reported one thousand cases of "active euthanasia without explicit request of the patient" in the Netherlands in 1990. Although it is not the whole of his argument, Herbert Hendin cites this as evidence that the Dutch guidelines for euthanasia are ignored by doctors. Euthanasia advocates contend that such cases occur in all nations, and that the Netherlands is simply the only one to study the problem and openly share the results. However, Robert Young also cites another, similar study that was conducted in 1995. Some of the data from the 1990 and 1995 studies are listed on a chart in the two-part viewpoint by Young and Orentlicher. In your opinion, do these data support the claim that the Dutch are on a "slippery slope"? Explain your answer.

CHAPTER 4

1. What is the principle of double effect, as described by Lonnie Bristow? Kenneth Cauthen claims that doctors often prescribe heavy doses of morphine in order to hasten the death of suffering patients, and then use the principle of double effect to protect themselves from legal persecution. Do you agree with the American Medical Association's assertion that the distinction between relieving pain and intending death is important in such cases, or do you agree with Cauthen's conclusion that society should accept "what is really going on"?

2. Leon Kass and Nelson Lund place great importance on the Hippocratic Oath, while Derek Humphry and Mary Clement believe its prohibition on physician-assisted suicide is a poor reason for opposing the practice. Do you believe, as Lund and Kass do, that a taboo on intentional killing is essential to the ethical practice of medicine, or do you agree with Humphry and Clement's claim that doctors should use their own judgment when faced with a request for suicide? Defend your answer.

ORGANIZATIONS TO CONTACT

The editors have compiled the following list of organizations concerned with the issues debated in this book. The descriptions are derived from materials provided by the organizations. All have publications or information available for interested readers. The list was compiled on the date of publication of the present volume; the information provided here may change. Be aware that many organizations take several weeks or longer to respond to inquiries, so allow as much time as possible.

American Civil Liberties Union (ACLU)
132 W. 43rd St., New York, NY 10036
(212) 994-9800
website: http://www.aclu.org
The ACLU champions the rights of individuals in right-to-die and euthanasia cases as well as in many other civil rights issues. The Foundation of the ACLU provides legal defense, research, and education. The organization publishes the quarterly *Civil Liberties* and various pamphlets, books, and position papers.

American Life League (ALL)
PO Box 1350, Stafford, VA 22555
(540) 659-4171 • fax: (540) 659-2586
website: http://www.all.org
The league believes that human life is sacred. It works to educate Americans about the dangers of all forms of euthanasia and opposes legislative efforts that would legalize or increase its incidence. It publishes the bimonthly pro-life magazine *Celebrate Life* and distributes videos, brochures, and newsletters monitoring euthanasia-related developments.

American Society of Law, Medicine, and Ethics
765 Commonwealth Ave., Suite 1634, Boston, MA 02215
(617) 262-4990 • fax: (617) 437-7596
e-mail: aslme@bu.edu • website: http://www.aslme.org
The society's members include physicians, attorneys, health care administrators, and others interested in the relationship between law, medicine, and ethics. The organization has an information clearinghouse and a library, and it acts as a forum for discussion of issues such as euthanasia and assisted suicide. It publishes the quarterlies *American Journal of Law and Medicine* and *Journal of Law, Medicine, and Ethics*, the newsletter *ASLME Briefings*, and books such as *Legal and Ethical Aspects of Treating Critically and Terminally Ill Patients*.

Choice in Dying (CID)
1035 30th Street NW, Washington, DC 20007
(800) 989-WILL (989-9455)
e-mail: cid@choices.org • website: http://www.choices.org

Choice in Dying is a national, not-for-profit organization dedicated to fostering communication about complex end-of-life decisions among individuals, their loved ones, and health care professionals. The organization invented living wills in 1967 and provides the only national hotline to respond to families and patients during end-of-life crises. CID also provides educational materials, public and professional education, and ongoing monitoring of changes in state and federal right-to-die legislation.

Citizens United Resisting Euthanasia (CURE, Ltd.)
812 Stephen St., Berkeley Springs, WV 25433
(304) 258-5433 • fax: (304) 258-5420
e-mail: CUREltd@ix.netcom.com
website: http://www.netcom.com/~cureltd

Founded in 1981, CURE is a nationwide network of concerned citizens of diverse professional, political, and religious backgrounds who oppose euthanasia. It provides advisors, research, and education. CURE publishes *Life Support* and *Dying Patient's Treatment* directives and *Life Matters* brochures.

Compassion in Dying Federation
6312 SW Capitol Hwy., Suite 415, Portland, OR 97201
(503) 221-9556 • fax: (503) 228-9610
e-mail: info@compassionindying.org
website: http://www.compassionindying.org

The mission of Compassion in Dying Federation is to provide national leadership for client service, legal advocacy, and public education to improve pain and symptom management, increase patient empowerment and self-determination, and expand end-of-life choices to include aid-in-dying for terminally ill, mentally competent adults.

Death with Dignity
520 South El Camino Real, Suite 710, San Mateo, CA 94402
(650) 344-6489 • fax: (650) 344-8100
e-mail: admin@deathwithdignity.org
website: http://www.deathwithdignity.org

Death with Dignity is a nonprofit charitable organization dedicated to increasing the choices and autonomy of terminally ill patients. The organization provides programs of education, and advocacy, and serves as an information resource for the public and the media. It publishes a variety of information, including the pamphlet *Choices at Life's End*.

Euthanasia Prevention Coalition BC
103-2609 Westview Drive, Suite 126, North Vancouver, BC V7N 4N2 CANADA
(604) 795-3772 • fax: (604) 794-3960
website: http://www.epc.bc.ca/

The Euthanasia Prevention Coalition opposes the promotion or legalization of euthanasia and assisted suicide. The coalition's purpose is to educate the public on risks associated with the promotion of euthanasia, increase public awareness of alternative methods for the relief of suffering, and to represent the vulnerable as an advocate before the courts on issues of euthanasia and related subjects. Press releases from the coalition are available at its website.

Euthanasia Research and Guidance Organization (ERGO!)
24829 Norris Lane, Junction City, OR 97448-9559
(541) 998-1873
e-mail: ergo@efn.org • website: http://www.finalexit.org

ERGO!, a nonprofit educational corporation, advocates physician-assisted dying for persons who are terminally or hopelessly ill and wish to end their suffering. As well as conducting opinion polls, ERGO! also develops and publishes guidelines for patients and physicians to better prepare them to make life-ending decisions. The organization's literature includes the quarterly *World Right-to-Die Newsletter*.

The Hemlock Society
PO Box 101810, Denver, CO 80250
(303) 639-1202 • (800) 247-7421 • fax: (303) 639-1224
e-mail: hemlock@privatei.com
website: http://www.hemlock.org/hemlock

The society believes that terminally ill individuals have the right to commit suicide. It publishes books on suicide, death, and dying, including *Final Exit*, a guide for those suffering with terminal illnesses and considering suicide. The Hemlock Society also publishes the newsletter *TimeLines*.

Human Life International (HLI)
4 Family Life Ln., Front Royal, VA 22630
(540) 635-7884 • fax: (540) 635-7363
e-mail: hli@hli.org • website: http://www.hli.org

HLI categorically rejects euthanasia and believes assisted suicide is morally unacceptable. It defends the rights of the unborn, the disabled, and those threatened by euthanasia; and it provides education, advocacy, and support services. HLI publishes the monthly newsletters *HLI Reports*, *HLI Update*, and *Deacons Circle*, as well as on-line articles on euthanasia.

International Anti-Euthanasia Task Force (IAETF)
PO Box 760, Steubenville, OH 43952
(740) 282-3810
e-mail: info@iaetf.org • website: http://www.iaetf.org

The task force opposes euthanasia, assisted suicide, and policies that threaten the lives of the medically vulnerable. IAETF publishes fact sheets and position papers on euthansia-related topics in addition to the bimonthly newsletter *IAETF Update*. It analyzes the policies and legislation concerning medical and social work organizations and files *amicus curiae* briefs in major "right-to-die" cases.

National Hospice Organization
1901 N. Moore Street, Suite 901, Arlington, VA 22209
(703) 243-5900 • (800) 658-8898 • fax: (703) 525-5762
e-mail: drsnho@cais.org • website: http://www.nho.org

The organization works to educate the public about the benefits of hospice care for the terminally ill and their families. Its members believe that with the proper care and pain medication, the terminally ill can live out their lives comfortably and in the company of their families. The organization opposes euthanasia and assisted suicide. It publishes the quarterlies *Hospice Journal* and *Hospice Magazine*, as well as books and monographs.

BIBLIOGRAPHY OF BOOKS

George J. Annas — *Some Choice: Law, Medicine, and the Market.* New York: Oxford University Press, 1998.

Michael Appleton et al. — *At Home with Terminal Illness: A Family Guide to Hospice in the Home.* Upper Saddle River, NJ: Prentice Hall, 1995.

Margaret P. Battin — *The Death Debate: Ethical Issues in Suicide.* Upper Saddle River, NJ: Prentice Hall, 1996.

Margaret P. Battin, Rosamond Rhodes, and Anita Silvers, eds. — *Physician-Assisted Suicide: Expanding the Debate.* New York: Routledge, 1998.

Tom L. Beauchamp, ed. — *Intending Death: The Ethics of Assisted Suicide and Euthanasia.* Upper Saddle River, NJ: Prentice Hall, 1996.

George M. Burnell — *Final Choices: To Live or Die in an Age of Medical Technology.* New York: Plenum, 1993.

Ira Byock — *Dying Well: Peace and Possibilities at the End of Life.* New York: Riverhead Books, 1997.

Committee on Medical Ethics, Episcopal Diocese of Washington, D.C. — *Assisted Suicide and Euthanasia: Christian Moral Perspectives: The Washington Report.* Harrisburg, PA: Morehouse, 1997.

Donald W. Cox — *Hemlock's Cup: The Struggle for Death with Dignity.* Amherst, NY: Prometheus Books, 1993.

David Cundiff — *Euthanasia Is Not the Answer: A Hospice Physician's View.* Totowa, NJ: Humana, 1992.

George E. Delury — *But What If She Wants to Die?: A Husband's Diary.* Secaucus, NJ: Birch Lane, 1997.

Timothy J. Demy and Gary P. Stewart, eds. — *Suicide: A Christian Response, Crucial Considerations for Choosing Life.* Grand Rapids, MI: Kregel, 1998.

Gerald Dworkin et al. — *Euthanasia and Physician Assisted Suicide.* New York: Cambridge University Press, 1998.

Ronald Dworkin — *Life's Dominion: An Argument About Abortion, Euthanasia, and Individual Freedom.* New York: Alfred A. Knopf, 1993.

Linda L. Emanuel, ed. — *Regulating How We Die: The Ethical, Medical, and Legal Issues Surrounding Physician-Assisted Suicide.* Cambridge, MA: Harvard University Press, 1998.

Peter G. Filene — *In the Arms of Others: A Cultural History of the Right-to-Die in America.* Chicago: Ivan R. Dee, 1998.

Sally B. Geis, ed. — *How Shall We Die?: Helping Christians Debate Assisted Suicide.* Nashville, TN: Abingdon, 1997.

Robin Gill, ed.	*Euthanasia and the Churches*. New York: Cassell Academic, 1998.
Carrie Gordon	*Prescribing Death: Euthanasia Exposed: The Right to Die or the Right to Kill?* Colorado Springs, CO: Focus on the Family, 1997.
Luke Gormally	*Euthanasia: Clinical Practice and the Law*. London: Linacre Centre, 1994.
John Griffiths et al.	*Euthanasia and Law in the Netherlands*. Ann Arbor: University of Michigan Press, 1998.
Joan K. Harrold and Joanne Lynn, eds.	*A Good Dying: Shaping Health Care for the Last Months of Life*. Binghamton, NY: Haworth, 1998.
Herbert Hendin	*Seduced by Death: Doctors, Patients, and the Dutch Cure*. New York: W.W. Norton, 1998.
James M. Hoefler	*Deathright: Culture, Medicine, Politics, and the Right to Die*. Boulder, CO: Westview, 1994.
Derek Humphry	*Final Exit: The Practicalities of Self-Deliverance and Assisted Suicide for the Dying*. Minneapolis: DTP Direct, 1997.
Derek Humphry and Mary Clement	*Freedom to Die: People, Politics, and the Right-to-Die Movement*. New York: St. Martin's, 1998.
Stephen Jamison	*Final Acts of Love: Families, Friends, and Assisted Dying*. New York: J.P. Tarcher, 1995.
Brian P. Johnston	*Death as a Salesman: What's Wrong with Assisted Suicide*. Sacramento, CA: New Regency, 1997.
John Keown, ed.	*Euthanasia Examined: Ethical, Clinical, and Legal Perspectives*. New York: Cambridge University Press, 1995.
Jack Kevorkian	*Prescription Medicide: The Goodness of Planned Death*. Amherst, NY: Prometheus Books, 1991.
Hans Kung et al.	*Dying with Dignity: A Plea for Personal Responsibility*. New York: Continuum, 1996.
Edward J. Larson and Darrel W. Amundsen, eds.	*A Different Death: Euthanasia in the Christian Tradition*. Downers Grove, IL: Intervarsity, 1998.
Gerald A. Larue	*Playing God: Fifty Religions' Views on Your Right to Die*. Wakefield, RI: Moyer Bell, 1996.
Marcia Lattanzi-Licht et al.	*The Hospice Choice: In Pursuit of a Peaceful Death*. New York: Fireside, 1998.
Michael Manning	*Euthanasia and Physician-Assisted Suicide: Killing or Caring?* Mahwah, NJ: Paulist, 1998.
Eric Marcus	*Why Suicide? Answers to 200 of the Most Frequently Asked Questions About Suicide, Attempted Suicide, and Assisted Suicide*. San Francisco: HarperSanFrancisco, 1996.

William F. May	*Testing the Medical Covenant: Active Euthanasia and Health Care Reform.* Grand Rapids, MI: William B. Eerdmans, 1996.
Jonathan D. Moreno	*Arguing Euthanasia: The Controversy over Mercy Killing.* New York: Simon & Schuster, 1995.
New York State Task Force of Life and the Law	*When Death Is Sought: Assisted Suicide and Euthanasia in the Medical Context.* New York State Department of Health, 1996. Available from http://www.health.state.ny.us/nysdoh/provider /death.htm.
M. Scott Peck	*Denial of the Soul: Spiritual and Medical Perspectives on Euthanasia and Mortality.* New York: Random House, 1997.
Carole Post et al.	*A Graceful Exit: Life and Death on Your Own Terms.* Menlo Park, CA: Insight Books, 1996.
Timothy E. Quill	*Death and Dignity: Making Choices and Taking Charge.* New York: W.W. Norton, 1993.
Lonny Shavelson	*A Chosen Death: The Dying Confront Assisted Suicide.* Berkeley and Los Angeles: University of California Press, 1998.
Wesley J. Smith	*Forced Exit: The Slippery Slope from Assisted Suicide to Legalized Murder.* New York: Times Books, 1997.
Bonnie Steinbock, ed.	*Killing and Letting Die.* New York: Fordham University Press, 1994.
David C. Thomasma, ed.	*Asking to Die: Inside the Dutch Debate About Euthanasia.* Norwell, MA: Kluwer Academic, 1998.
Michael M. Uhlmann, ed.	*Last Rights?: Assisted Suicide and Euthanasia Debated.* Grand Rapids, MI: William B. Eerdmans, 1998.
Michael Vitez	*Final Choices: Seeking the Good Death.* Philadelphia: Camino Books, 1998.
Robert F. Weir	*Ethical Issues in Suicide.* Upper Saddle River, NJ: Prentice Hall, 1995.
Robert F. Weir, ed.	*Physician-Assisted Suicide.* Bloomington: Indiana University Press, 1997.
James L. Werth	*Rational Suicide?: Implications for Mental Health Professionals.* Bristol, PA: Taylor & Francis, 1996.
James L. Werth, ed.	*Contemporary Perspectives on Rational Suicide.* Levittown, PA: Brunner/Mazel, 1998.
Sue Woodman	*Last Rights: The Struggle over the Right to Die.* New York: Plenum, 1998.

INDEX

abortion, 41, 70, 121
  is convenient for women, 123
  is forbidden by Hippocratic oath, 183
  is leading to euthanasia, 183–84
advance directives, 75, 141, 156, 184
African Americans, 130, 137
AIDS patients, 73, 74, 173
Alexander, Leo, 128–29, 130
American Disabled for Attendant
  Programs Today (ADAPT), 140, 142
American Journal of Hospice and Palliative Care, 109
American Medical Association, 164, 171
  on hospice care, 99, 102
  is out of sync with physicians, 178–80
  opposes assisted suicide, 151, 167–68,
    173, 174, 179, 184
  physicians disagree with, 173
  on starvation and dehydration, 146
Americans with Disabilities Act, 134, 140
Angell, Marcia, 46
Annas, George, 98
anti-Semitism, 131–32
assisted suicide, 56, 59
  and the abortion debate, 41, 183–84
  of AIDS patients, 173
  cannot be regulated, 81–82
  compared to euthanasia, 48, 56
  of disabled people, 134
  does not violate medical tradition, 176
  Hemlock Society's view of, 140–42
  is a crime, 18, 20, 48
  is always wrong, 28, 29, 34–35, 37
  is compassionate act, 21, 163, 164, 165
  is ethical practice for physicians, 162–65
  is greater danger than treatment
    withdrawal, 84–85
  is incorrect terminology, 110
  is morally acceptable, 52, 58–59, 110
  is not a cost-cutting measure, 76
  is not patient's right, 99
  is performed by U.S. doctors, 74, 76,
    81–82, 111, 173
  is progressive social cause, 134, 137
  is slowly being accepted by medical
    establishment, 178–79
  laws against, 35, 50, 51, 70
  must be regulated, 76–77
  must be seen from patient's perspective,
    53
  for nonterminal illnesses, 86
  opposition to, 42, 151, 167–68, 173,
    174, 179, 184

  public opinion on, 72, 73, 91, 111,
    164, 184
  requests withdrawn for, 79, 148
  should be an option, 45, 51–52, 109
  should be legalized, 71–77
  should not be legalized, 79–87
  will replace palliative care, 149
  vs. withholding/withdrawing
    treatment, 169
  see also euthanasia; physician-assisted
    suicide laws; physicians; right-to-die
    movement; terminally ill people
Assisted Suicide Funding Restriction Act,
  102
Atlantic Monthly, 83
Auschwitz concentration camps, 131
Australia, 57, 65, 156
  Rights of the Terminally Ill Act in, 71
autonomy. *See* self-determination
autopsies, 20

Baron, Charles, 80, 178
Batavia, Andrew, 73
Battin, Margaret P., 52
Bell, Karen, 103
Bernardin, Joseph, 38, 95
Berry, Patricia, 100
Beschle, Donald, 80–81
bigotry, 125–26, 135
Bioethics, 90
Bouvia, Elizabeth, 153
Bristow, Lonnie R., 166
British Medical Journal, 179–80
Buddhism, 107–108
Byock, Ira, 37, 98, 101, 102, 103

California, 64, 111, 151, 168
  living will law in, 70
  Proposition 161 in, 71
Callahan, Daniel, 81, 130
Canada, 61
Caplan, Arthur, 179
carbon monoxide gas, 56–57
Catholics
  on euthanasia, 26, 34–39, 71
  on moral obligations regarding illness,
    26
  on pain management, 36
  on quantity vs. quality of life issues, 74
  on withholding medical treatment, 25,
    26
  see also Christians

is effective, 101
is not always effective, 76, 101, 109, 151, 168
for poor and minorities, 60
right to, 62–63
sedation as, 108, 109
see also lethal medications; morphine
palliative care, 97–99, 101, 106–109, 148–49
can control pain, 168
in the Netherlands, 147
research on, 101–102
will be replaced by assisted suicide, 149
see also hospice care
patients. *See* terminally ill people
Patient Self-Determination Act, 141
patients' rights movement, 141, 176
see also right-to-die movement
Peck, M. Scott, 100
physician-assisted suicide laws, 23
are a sign of society's failure, 171
are unconstitutional, 35, 50, 51, 70
attempts at, 70–71
under due process/equal protection clauses, 50, 82–84, 112, 144
cannot be limited to the terminally ill, 85–86
cannot protect patients, 81–82
hospice care as alternative to, 97–100, 102, 104, 107, 108
is not helpful argument, 109
must require patient's participation, 49, 51, 73, 110, 152–53
need countercontrols, 129–30
only for the terminally ill, 153
in Oregon, 18, 23, 25, 57, 64–65, 71, 97, 151
safeguards may be disregarded, 152
safeguards must prevent abuse, 142
safeguards will not be effective, 169
safeguards will prevent abuse in, 156–57
through evaluations by psychiatrists, 152
through provision of palliative care, 152
through second opinions, 153
through use of state legislatures, 153
through use of the courts, 153
"safe lethal dose" in, 25
slippery slope arguments on, 44, 50–51, 75, 95, 110, 121, 125–28, 169–70
are logical, 123
are not inevitable, 154–55
are unethical and undemocratic, 126–27

are unpersuasive, 50, 127
do not apply to Nazi Germany, 130–32
do not apply to the Netherlands, 155–56
and the double effect principle, 189
economics in, 50, 126
rest on fatalistic assumptions, 127
validated by Nazi Germany, 125, 128–29, 154, 155
validated in the Netherlands, 144, 154
will be prevented by legal constraints, 76, 125, 127
will be prevented by social restraints, 126
support for, 71–77, 173–74, 179
will be broken by doctors, 148
will be civil rights violations, 136
will cause doctors to lose autonomy, 178
will destroy patients' control, 145, 147
will enhance patient-physician relationship, 74
will give patients more control, 178
will harm the disabled, 134–36, 137–38
will increase unethical behavior in doctors, 182–83, 185–90
will kill vulnerable people, 57, 58, 64, 73, 81, 126, 151
will lead to abuse, 58, 60–61, 118–23, 126–27
will lessen doctors' care, 185–87
will not be effective, 169
will not harm the disabled, 141
will not lead to involuntary killing, 128–32
will overturn medical taboos, 182, 184–85
will undermine patient-physician relationship, 167
will victimize the poor, 169–70
will work in a democracy, 128, 130, 132
see also assisted suicide; Netherlands, assisted suicide guidelines in
physicians, 72
act on nonmedical judgments, 187
as agents of death, 71–72, 188, 190
ancient Hippocratic, 182–83
are not taught hospice care, 98
are taught repugnance to killing, 187, 189
are taught to care for dying, 187–88
can ethically increase pain medication, 168–69
can ethically practice assisted suicide, 162–65